Copyright © 2024 Andrea Oliver

All rights reserved

The characters and events portrayed in this book are fictitious. Any similarity to real persons, living or dead, is coincidental and not intended by the author.

No part of this book may be reproduced, or stored in a retrieval system, or transmitted in any form or by any means, electronic, mechanical, photocopying, recording, or otherwise, without express written permission of the publisher.

Cover design by: Art Painter
Library of Congress Control Number: 2018675309
Printed in the United States of America

CONTENTS

Copyright
Introduction — 2
Chapter 1: — 6
Chapter 2: The Characteristics of a Gold Rush Economy — 17
Chapter 3: Seeing Around Corners — 24
Chapter 4: The Importance of Mindset and Resilience — 31
Chapter 5: Developing a Unique Value Proposition — 38
Chapter 6: Building Networks and Resources — 45
Chapter 7: The First-Mover Advantage and Its Risks — 54
Chapter 8: The Power of Supporting Industries — 61
Chapter 9: Scaling and Diversifying as the Market Matures — 69
Chapter 10: Innovate or Get Left Behind — 78
Chapter 11: Investing in Future-Based Markets — 86
Chapter 12: Building Resilient Wealth — 94
Conclusion: Key Takeaways from the Gold Rush — 102
Appendix — 105

ANDREA. OLIVER

Lessons From The Gold Rush That Can Make You Rich Today

INTRODUCTION

Let's cut to the chase: if getting rich was as simple as waking up one day, declaring "I'm going to be rich!" and waiting for the money to roll in, well... we'd all be sipping cocktails on private islands by now. "Overnight" success is a wonderful myth, but that's all it is—a myth. The truth is, creating wealth, especially the kind that lasts, takes a bit more finesse. And the good news? You don't need to be born into it, you don't need a million-dollar idea, and you certainly don't need a miracle. What you do need is the skill of spotting and seizing opportunities, and the nerve to act when everyone around you is saying, "Are you crazy?"

So, where does that "overnight" success narrative really come from? Here's the secret: when people say "overnight," they're often skipping the part where someone put in days, months, or even years of work before their big break came. And those who didn't? They got extremely lucky, and honestly, relying on luck is a terrible business plan. Real "overnight" success? It's the ability to spot what others can't see yet, taking action when the opportunity arises, and doing so with unwavering confidence—especially when people tell you you're nuts.

The Real Reason Opportunities Go Unseen

Here's the thing about opportunities: they're not invisible, but they might as well be. They don't come with neon signs saying, "Hey, look over here! Riches await!" If they did, we'd all have panned for gold by now. The truth is, opportunities go unnoticed because they often look suspiciously like hard work, insane risks, or—worse yet—a waste of time and resources. And thanks to a little thing called societal skepticism, most people run in the opposite direction when something looks too good to be true. Instead, they cling to the "safe" path because that's what the world tells them is "smart."

This book is about helping you see through that cloud of doubt. To turn opportunities into reality, you've got to look at things differently. You have to train yourself to see patterns that hint at something bigger, to lean in when others back away, and to believe in your vision when nobody else does. I won't lie to you—some people are going to think you've lost it. But remember, it's the same routine every time a Gold Rush happens: skeptics doubt, pioneers take the plunge, and those who recognize the signs early are the ones who cash in. And here's the beauty: you can be one of those people. You just have to train your eye to spot the next Gold Rush before it turns into the next... whatever that hot thing is everyone's raving about on the morning news.

Why *This* Time Is Different

If you're here, it means you're ready to learn what it takes to catch that next big wave—and this time, it's no longer about finding gold in a river. Today's Gold Rushes don't involve pickaxes and pans but rather innovations, technology, and smart moves that seem obvious only in hindsight. In fact, today's Gold Rushes are often hidden in plain sight, in the businesses, industries, and trends the world's just beginning to notice.

We're in an era of change, and this time, we don't need wagons or creeks. The playing field is open, and the internet, global markets, and technology mean anyone, including you, can find a spot. It's not about having a perfect map or foolproof plan; it's about seeing what others miss and acting on it. If you're willing to shake off those "overnight" expectations and dive in with both feet, then this book is your guide to understanding how it all works—so you can make your move the next time you hear whispers of a "Gold

Rush."

Are you ready to be the one with a shovel when the rest are waiting for a map? Good. Because this isn't just another book about wealth; it's your invitation to see the world differently, to find opportunities where others see dead ends, and to stop waiting for an "overnight" that never comes.

Let's get digging.

Part I: Recognizing Modern-Day Gold Rushes

CHAPTER 1:

The History of Gold Rushes — Lessons in Opportunity

If there's one thing history has taught us, it's this: the quickest way to get everyone's attention is to say the words "gold" and "rush" in the same sentence. You say "gold," and you'll get a raised eyebrow. Add "rush," and suddenly everyone within earshot has packed a suitcase and is heading to the nearest creek. There's something magnetic about the idea that hidden riches are out there, just waiting to be claimed. And while the gold itself is appealing, what really captivates people is the *opportunity*—the promise of finding something that can change your life in a moment, that elusive idea of "overnight" wealth.

But here's where it gets interesting: every Gold Rush is built on the same basic pattern, and it's a pattern that repeats over and over again in different forms, right up to the present day. Once you understand that, you can start spotting the next big Gold Rush before everyone else—whether it's in a tech startup, a new industry, or a market trend just waiting to explode. So, let's take a journey back in time and explore two of the biggest Gold Rushes in American history: the North Carolina Gold Rush and the California Gold Rush. Not only did they create immense wealth, but they also left behind lessons in opportunity that still apply today. Ready to dig in?

The North Carolina Gold Rush — A Nugget of Wealth, 1803

Let's set the scene: North Carolina, early 1800s. A twelve-year-old boy named Conrad Reed is fishing on his family's farm. He notices a glimmering rock in the creek, hauls it out, and brings it back home. Now, if Conrad's parents had known what they were looking at, they would've probably thrown the rock a welcome party. But instead, they used it as a doorstop for three years. *Three years!* That rock, which they casually kicked every time they opened the door, turned out to be a 17-pound gold nugget. That's right—Conrad had stumbled onto what would eventually spark the first U.S. Gold Rush, right in the middle of North Carolina.

Now, you might think, "How could anyone be so oblivious?" But that's the thing about opportunities. They don't usually show up with "Hey, I'm valuable!" written on them in neon. Most people, like Conrad's family, don't recognize them because they're disguised as ordinary. But for the people who are paying attention, they're the ticket to fortune.

So, once word got out that there was gold in North Carolina, people rushed in, tools in hand, ready to dig. However, the real winners of this Gold Rush weren't always the ones who found the nuggets. The true wealth was often made by those who saw an opportunity to supply the rushers—selling shovels, pans, and supplies to the miners, who had traveled miles and miles with nothing but their hopes and dreams. As more gold was found, new businesses popped up, and suddenly, North Carolina was a hub of economic activity. The ripple effect transformed the local economy, creating an entire industry around mining, refining, and trading gold. And, just like that, wealth wasn't just being mined—it was being *created*.

But eventually, as more people flooded in, the easy-to-find gold disappeared. Mining got tougher, competition got stiffer, and those late to the game found themselves scraping the bottom of the creek. By the time they arrived, the Gold Rush was already drying up. And here's Lesson #1 from the North Carolina Gold Rush:

Opportunities are ripe for those who arrive early and prepared. Once you hear about it in the news, the Gold Rush has already begun, and by the time everyone's talking about it, it's often winding down.

The California Gold Rush — Gold Fever Goes West, 1848

Fast forward a few decades to 1848. James W. Marshall, a carpenter working at Sutter's Mill in California, notices something glinting in the American River. He picks it up, tests it, and yep—it's gold. What Marshall and his employer, John Sutter, don't know is that this little discovery is about to kick off one of the biggest mass migrations in history. Within a year, over 300,000 people would head to California, hoping to strike it rich. And here's the kicker: most of them wouldn't find gold at all.

Now, if you've read anything about the California Gold Rush, you've probably heard of the "49ers." These were the folks who flooded California in 1849 after hearing about the initial discovery. They came from all over—from the East Coast, from Europe, even from China. They risked everything: some sold their farms, others spent their life savings, and still more just up and left, betting it all on the hope of wealth. It's like a live-action version of "Who Wants to Be a Millionaire?" except instead of answering questions, they're hacking through mountains and panning rivers.

But here's where things get interesting: the people who became the wealthiest during the California Gold Rush weren't the ones finding gold. No, the biggest winners were the ones supplying the miners. That's right—the folks selling shovels, boots, coffee, and even whiskey made a killing. Samuel Brannan, for instance, didn't just cash in—he practically minted money. He famously bought up every pickaxe, pan, and shovel he could find, and then ran through the streets shouting, "Gold! Gold from the American River!" while selling supplies at a markup. People like Brannan made fortunes not by finding gold but by seeing the opportunity to *support* those who were.

It's a classic Gold Rush lesson that has replayed itself time and time again: **you don't need to be the one striking gold to strike it rich. Sometimes the real money is in supporting those who are trying.** Fast-forward to today, and you'll find this same pattern in modern Gold Rushes. Think about the rise of e-commerce: Amazon became a behemoth not by finding "gold" but by providing the infrastructure for people to buy and sell. And that brings us to Lesson #2: **If you can't be the pioneer, be the one making their journey possible.**

The Gold Rush Framework — A Repeatable Pattern for Wealth Creation

So, what do these Gold Rushes have in common, and why does it matter? The answer is simple: they all follow a pattern, and it's a pattern that repeats itself in different industries, economies, and technologies. And if you know how to recognize it, you can start spotting these Gold Rushes before everyone else. Let's break it down.

1. **Skepticism and Doubt**
   Every Gold Rush begins with doubt. The first people to hear about it say, "Gold in North Carolina? Please. That's as likely as unicorns." But then, as a few brave souls start finding success, others start to believe. This skepticism is key because it creates an early window for those willing to take the plunge. Lesson: When you hear skeptics, lean in and ask yourself if they're right—or if they just can't see the opportunity yet.
2. **Proof of Concept**
   Once someone strikes gold, people take notice. Proof of concept is powerful; it flips the switch from "impossible" to "maybe possible." In the California Gold Rush, the news didn't spread instantly, but once it did, it was

game on. This stage is your sign to pay attention—early adopters are often the ones who make the most significant gains because they're positioned before the masses.

3. **Mass Entry and the Gold Rush Stage**
   Now comes the mad dash. At this point, everyone from farmers to city slickers starts heading west (or, in today's case, jumping into whatever new industry is trending). But remember: the early birds tend to get the best worms. If you're not early, you'll need to think creatively to get ahead. This stage is where supporting businesses and service providers can thrive by meeting the needs of the masses.

4. **The Rise of Support Industries**
   As more people enter the market, the need for supplies and services skyrockets. This is the stage where those who aren't directly involved in finding the "gold" start making a fortune. The people selling shovels, tents, and provisions during the Gold Rush didn't need to mine to strike it rich. Today, this might mean offering services, tools, or technology to support a booming industry.

5. **Innovation and Specialization**
   Eventually, the field gets crowded. The Gold Rush in California became so competitive that traditional mining gave way to hydraulic mining—an expensive, high-tech method that only well-funded companies could afford. As a result, small-time miners were squeezed out. This stage tells us that to stay in the game, you have to innovate or specialize. Those who can adapt to new conditions thrive, while those who can't get left behind.

6. **Permanent Change in the Ecosystem**
   Once a Gold Rush has run its course, the effects don't disappear—they leave a lasting impact. The California Gold Rush, for example, transformed the state into

an economic powerhouse and permanently altered its population, economy, and infrastructure. Every Gold Rush creates a new "normal," and those who are part of it help shape the future. This stage is a reminder that when you find a Gold Rush, you're not just chasing wealth—you're part of something bigger, a wave that leaves a legacy.

This six-step framework isn't just history—it's a blueprint for recognizing today's and tomorrow's Gold Rushes. Once you can spot these stages, you'll start seeing opportunities everywhere, from tech booms to sustainable energy to emerging markets. Every time a new trend surfaces, it's just a matter of time before the Gold Rush begins.

The real lesson here? Gold Rushes don't end—they just change form. And while there might not be nuggets in your backyard, there are plenty of opportunities waiting for you to grab a shovel, dive in, and start digging for your own version of gold. So, what do you say? Ready to be the one who sees opportunity when others just see dirt?

Skepticism and Doubt — The Hidden Gift of Early Doubts

If you had lived in North Carolina in 1803 or California in 1848, hearing rumors of gold would probably have sounded as credible as someone telling you they found a winning lottery ticket just lying on the street. And if you were practical, you might have brushed it off and gone about your day. This is the power—and the paradox—of skepticism. In the early days of every Gold Rush, doubt creates a unique opportunity. The fewer people who believe, the fewer there are to compete with.

The first stage of any Gold Rush is almost always met with skepticism, and for good reason: every big idea, every shift, every wealth-building innovation starts out as a bit of a gamble. In

North Carolina, when young Conrad Reed first showed people his golden "doorstop," no one thought much of it. Then, even after a few more findings, people still doubted it was worth their time or energy to go gold-hunting. It was only after word spread beyond the local area that the true frenzy began.

In modern times, skepticism often surfaces as something more subtle—like dismissing new technology or a "fad" market. When Amazon first started selling books online, people thought it was an impractical venture. And yet, a few believers (including early investors) recognized something others didn't: the power of e-commerce. They invested early, and the rest is history. Today, those who took that "ridiculous" gamble in Amazon's infancy are reaping the rewards in ways that were unimaginable back then.

The takeaway here? **If you only move when something is 100% accepted and "safe," you're already too late.** Skepticism is like a fog that keeps the masses at bay, while the few willing to push through the haze find themselves standing in a field of untapped potential. When you hear people dismissing an idea as a "crazy fad," lean in and do some digging. There might be a gold nugget under all that doubt.

Proof of Concept — When "Impossible" Becomes "Maybe"

There's something magical about the moment a Gold Rush becomes real. When one person hits gold, or one company takes off, everything changes. This is the "proof of concept" stage, and it's the tipping point when "impossible" transforms into "maybe."

Take the California Gold Rush, for example. James Marshall's first discovery of gold was a lonely event. There was no immediate crowd of onlookers, no flurry of excitement, and no stampede. But soon after the word got out and enough people found nuggets of their own, California was buzzing with hopeful miners from all over the world.

In today's world, this proof-of-concept stage often comes in the form of a startup or early adopter successfully implementing a new idea. Think of electric vehicles. Not too long ago, the idea of an electric car was considered both impractical and highly niche—more of a sci-fi dream than a practical mode of transportation. But then Tesla happened. By the time Tesla proved that electric cars weren't just possible but desirable, the game changed. Now, every major automaker is in the race to produce electric vehicles, and Tesla's stockholders are laughing all the way to the bank.

This is Lesson #2 of the Gold Rush framework: **Once someone has proved it works, the race begins.** If you're in early enough to witness the proof-of-concept stage, pay close attention. At this point, skeptics start turning into believers, and demand for this newfound opportunity begins to grow. It's a sign to dig in deeper, refine your approach, and position yourself as an early player before the big crowd arrives.

Mass Entry and the Gold Rush Stage — Where the Frenzy Begins

Once an opportunity reaches the proof-of-concept stage, the Gold Rush begins in earnest. This is when the masses jump in, lured by the success stories of the early movers. In California, this looked like thousands upon thousands of people traveling by ship, wagon, and horseback, enduring unbelievable hardships just for the chance to find a nugget of gold. In fact, California's population nearly quadrupled during the Gold Rush, creating the city of San Francisco practically overnight.

But here's the thing: by the time the big crowd shows up, the playing field changes. The easy gold is gone, and what remains requires a lot more work. At this stage, competition is fierce, and those who haven't arrived prepared are in for a rude awakening. For the savvy entrepreneur, though, this can be the golden stage—because this is when you can pivot to supporting the "rushers" instead of being one of them.

In today's Gold Rushes, this could look like entering a booming market that others are flocking to, but with a twist. Think about the rise of digital marketing. As companies scrambled to establish their online presence, a new industry emerged to support them: SEO services, content marketing, social media management, and more. The "Gold Rush" wasn't in just building an online store; it was in providing the tools and knowledge to *run* that store.

The lesson? **When the crowd arrives, don't fight the masses—support them.** This is your chance to pivot from "gold seeker" to "gold supplier." Instead of competing with everyone else, look for ways to add value to their journey.

The Rise of Support Industries — When Selling Shovels Becomes Lucrative

By the time the crowd gets settled and starts working, demand for supplies skyrockets. In the California Gold Rush, this meant that everything—shovels, picks, pans, boots, food—was suddenly a hot commodity. Those who couldn't find gold often made a fortune selling essentials to those who were still searching. Some of the most famous figures in Gold Rush history, like Levi Strauss, who began selling sturdy workwear to miners, made fortunes this way.

This stage in the framework is often where hidden opportunities lie. It's easy to think that the only way to wealth is by "finding gold," but in reality, the support businesses—the ones providing the "shovels" for others—often build wealth with far more stability and longevity.

Today, this might mean offering specialized tools, services, or resources to new industries. When crypto took off, companies providing exchange platforms, wallet services, and even educational resources about blockchain technology made significant profits. They weren't "mining" crypto—they were providing the picks and shovels. And as long as there's interest in a new field, the support industries will continue to thrive, often long after the initial rush is over.

Innovation and Specialization — Separating the Pioneers from the Followers

Eventually, every Gold Rush starts to mature. In California, as the years went by, the easy-to-find gold became scarce, forcing miners to adopt more advanced techniques. This led to the introduction of hydraulic mining, which required specialized equipment, more significant capital, and new expertise. At this point, the playing field changes once again. Small-time miners can't compete with big operations that have the resources to innovate.

The same is true in modern markets. Once an industry matures, it's no longer about being the first; it's about being the best. Companies need to specialize, innovate, or diversify to stay relevant. Consider how Netflix transformed from a DVD rental service into a streaming powerhouse. By the time other companies caught onto the idea of streaming, Netflix was already innovating with its own original content, setting itself apart from new entrants.

Here's where Lesson #5 comes in: **To keep thriving in a maturing market, you need to innovate or specialize.** At this stage, companies that survive are those that find new ways to add value. Whether it's by offering something unique or advancing the technology, this is where you separate the true industry leaders from the followers.

Permanent Change in the Ecosystem — The Legacy of a Gold Rush

Once a Gold Rush has run its course, the effects are long-lasting. California, once a sparsely populated area, was transformed into a bustling state. The infrastructure built during the Gold Rush—the towns, the roads, the economy—remained long after the gold had disappeared. This final stage reminds us that every major opportunity leaves a legacy, shaping the economy, culture, and landscape for years to come.

In today's world, you can see this effect in almost every major industry that's experienced a Gold Rush-like boom. The internet boom of the 2000s created the foundations for our current tech-driven economy, reshaping everything from how we work to how we socialize. Now, e-commerce is a daily norm, digital marketing is a must-have for any business, and our entire infrastructure is intertwined with the internet.

Lesson #6? **True Gold Rushes don't just create wealth; they reshape the landscape.** If you can be part of a Gold Rush, whether by finding gold, supplying it, or innovating within it, you're not just making money—you're contributing to something larger, something that will define the future.

Bringing It All Together — Recognizing the Patterns of Wealth Creation

So, there it is—the Gold Rush framework in all its glory. From North Carolina to California, from skepticism to legacy, these six stages of opportunity creation repeat themselves over and over. Once you know how to spot them, you'll start seeing opportunities everywhere. You'll understand why early doubters are sometimes your best friends, how to pivot from competition to support, and when it's time to innovate or specialize.

Gold Rushes are no longer limited to nuggets in a river or silver in a mine. Today, they're in industries like clean energy, artificial intelligence, biotech, and more. And now that you have the framework, you're ready to start finding the next Gold Rush and make your own way. So grab your shovel—or better yet, start selling them—and let's get to work on creating your own legacy.

CHAPTER 2: THE CHARACTERISTICS OF A GOLD RUSH ECONOMY

So, you're ready to dig into the world of wealth creation and start identifying the next big opportunity. But let's get one thing straight: not every market or trend is a Gold Rush. Just because something is popular, trending, or sounds glamorous doesn't mean it's ripe with life-changing potential. A true Gold Rush economy is something different—a perfect storm where the right combination of factors creates an unprecedented chance for wealth creation. Knowing how to spot these factors is your golden ticket.

In this chapter, we're going to break down the essential ingredients of a Gold Rush market. We'll take a look at unexplored or unregulated markets, emerging technologies, and unmet needs, then bring these concepts to life with case studies, both historical and modern. By the end, you'll be able to spot the signs of a Gold Rush brewing, even if it's wrapped up in buzzwords and hype.

Key Indicators of a Gold Rush Market

When we talk about a "Gold Rush market," we're talking about a unique set of characteristics that set the stage for extraordinary opportunities. Here's what to look for:

LESSONS FROM THE GOLD RUSH THAT CAN MAKE YOU RICH TODAY

1. **Unexplored or Unregulated Markets**
    - The most fertile ground for a Gold Rush is often uncharted territory. Think of it like an undiscovered island or a blank canvas where anything seems possible. These markets are typically either unexplored or unregulated, which means the playing field is as level as it's going to get, and anyone with a vision can jump in.
2. **New Technologies and Innovations**
    - New technology doesn't just create new products; it often creates entire new industries. Think of the internet in the 1990s or smartphones in the late 2000s. When a technology is groundbreaking enough, it reshapes consumer behavior, market demand, and the way business is done. If you're lucky enough to spot a Gold Rush in this area, you're not just catching a wave—you're surfing it.
3. **Unmet Needs and High Demand**
    - Every Gold Rush has a driving need behind it. In California, it was the promise of gold. With the internet, it was a newfound demand for instant information and connectivity. And with clean energy today, it's the urgent need to find sustainable solutions. Gold Rush economies thrive when there's a high demand for something that people can't get enough of.
4. **Low Initial Competition but Potential for Rapid Saturation**
    - In the beginning, a Gold Rush market is relatively open. There's room to grow, and you're

not elbowing your way through a packed crowd. But as soon as people catch on, it starts to fill up fast. Knowing how to spot that initial gap—and how to pivot when saturation hits—is the key to staying profitable.

5. **Room for Supporting Industries and Innovations**
   - We've already covered how it's often the people selling the shovels who make the most money in a Gold Rush. A true Gold Rush economy creates space for supportive businesses, whether they're providing tools, training, or related services.

Now that you know what to look for, let's bring these ideas to life with some real-world examples.

Case Study #1: The Internet Boom — Building the Digital Gold Mine

The internet didn't start as a Gold Rush; it started as a geeky novelty. In the early '80s, people saw it as something only for scientists or tech nerds. But by the '90s, when websites started popping up and businesses realized they could sell things online, the Internet Boom took off like wildfire. Suddenly, everyone from small mom-and-pop shops to massive corporations was scrambling to establish an online presence.

The Opportunity: Early adopters like Amazon, Yahoo, and eBay weren't just experimenting with new technology—they were creating a whole new way of life. The internet boom brought with it a massive unmet need for connectivity, information, and convenience. Early internet pioneers saw an unexplored market with virtually no competition, and they took full advantage.

The Result: The companies that entered early—whether by building e-commerce sites, offering online advertising, or creating digital infrastructure—have largely become household names.

Amazon started out by selling books online, but it wasn't long before they expanded into a full-fledged e-commerce giant. Early investors in these companies, like venture capitalists who believed in Jeff Bezos' crazy idea to sell books over the internet, made fortunes that are still growing today.

Lesson Learned: The internet was a Gold Rush market because it was new, unregulated, and driven by an undeniable need for information and access. If you had spotted this trend early on, you didn't even have to be the next Bezos. You could have built a web-hosting company, sold domain names, or offered digital marketing services. The point? A Gold Rush market is a whole ecosystem of opportunity.

Case Study #2: The Smartphone Revolution — The World in Your Pocket

In the early 2000s, the world of mobile technology was in its awkward teenage phase. We had phones, sure, but they were clunky, limited, and not exactly "smart." Then came Apple with the iPhone in 2007, and suddenly, mobile technology wasn't just about calling or texting—it was about having the internet, music, games, and social media all in one place.

The Opportunity: Apple's iPhone didn't just revolutionize phones; it created a massive Gold Rush market. Suddenly, there was a demand for apps, accessories, and a whole new wave of mobile-first businesses. This wasn't just about selling phones—it was about the entire ecosystem surrounding the smartphone.

The Result: The App Store, launched in 2008, was a game-changer. Developers around the world jumped in, creating apps for everything from productivity to social media. Companies like Instagram, WhatsApp, and Uber owe their entire existence to the smartphone revolution. Meanwhile, accessory companies began selling phone cases, screen protectors, chargers, and anything else you could possibly need for your new device.

Lesson Learned: Sometimes a Gold Rush isn't about the product itself but the ecosystem it creates. The smartphone revolution was a Gold Rush because it spurred an entire industry to support the main product. If you'd jumped in early—by developing an app, selling accessories, or even offering mobile tech support—you would have been riding one of the biggest Gold Rush waves of the 21st century.

Case Study #3: Clean Energy — The Power Shift

Today's Gold Rush is happening in the world of clean energy. With climate change becoming an increasingly urgent issue, there's a massive push for renewable energy sources like solar, wind, and hydrogen. Unlike past Gold Rushes, which were driven by novelty or convenience, clean energy is being driven by necessity. The world simply can't keep relying on fossil fuels, and that's creating a huge demand for alternatives.

The Opportunity: Renewable energy companies are at the forefront of this Gold Rush. But it's not just about the big names—there's room for companies offering supporting technologies, from energy storage to smart grid solutions, as well as smaller companies installing solar panels or developing new battery technologies.

The Result: In 2020, Tesla became the world's most valuable car company, largely due to its position as a leader in electric vehicles and clean energy. Meanwhile, companies specializing in solar panels, wind turbines, and even small-scale battery innovations are seeing their stocks soar. Governments are also incentivizing clean energy, creating even more opportunities for savvy entrepreneurs.

Lesson Learned: The clean energy market is booming because of an urgent unmet need and a high demand for sustainable solutions. With many countries offering incentives for renewable energy, the barriers to entry are lower than ever. For an entrepreneur, this means a Gold Rush opportunity, whether you're building solar panels, offering energy storage solutions, or simply selling to the companies at the forefront of the movement.

Tying It All Together — Your Guide to Spotting the Next Gold Rush

So, how do you take these lessons and apply them to the future? It's all about keeping an eye out for the key characteristics we covered earlier. Here's a quick guide to spotting the next Gold Rush:

1. **Look for Unexplored Markets**: Keep an ear to the ground for markets that are new, uncharted, or still in the "is this a thing?" phase. This is where opportunities lie for those willing to take a risk before the masses catch on.
2. **Watch for Emerging Technologies**: If a technology has the power to change the way we live, work, or play, there's a good chance it'll create a Gold Rush market. Blockchain, AI, and quantum computing are all technologies to keep an eye on.
3. **Find High-Demand, Unmet Needs**: Ask yourself, "What's something people really need that they can't get right now?" This question has led to the creation of entire industries, from e-commerce to ride-sharing to renewable energy.
4. **Enter Before the Market Saturates**: If you're getting in at the proof-of-concept stage, you're in a prime position to take advantage of low competition. But once saturation hits, it's time to pivot or specialize.
5. **Consider the Supporting Industries**: Remember, you don't have to be the main act to make money. Sometimes, the real wealth lies in supporting the Gold Rush with tools, services, or resources.

Final Thoughts on Spotting Gold Rushes

At the end of the day, a Gold Rush economy is about far more than just the "gold." It's about being able to see the potential in an uncharted market, understanding the ripple effects of new technologies, and creating solutions for unmet needs. The best part? You don't need to be a tech genius or a billionaire to spot the next Gold Rush. You just need a keen eye, a bit of courage, and the ability to see opportunity where others see chaos.

Now that you've got the basics down, you're ready to start looking at the world differently. Next time you hear about a new technology, a budding market, or a pressing global need, ask yourself: *Is this the next Gold Rush?* Because the answer just might surprise you.

CHAPTER 3: SEEING AROUND CORNERS

Welcome to the realm of seeing around corners, where fortune favors the visionary rather than the lucky. Imagine having the ability to see trends before everyone else does—like spotting a spark that others overlook, or hearing whispers of a trend long before it's shouted from every rooftop. That's the art of predicting emerging markets, and it's an art worth mastering if you want to dive into the next Gold Rush before everyone else.

In this chapter, we're going to talk about practical strategies for honing your instincts, developing an eye for trends, and seeing around corners. Think of it as building your sixth sense for market shifts—one that combines intuition, observation, and analysis. By the end, you'll have a toolkit for sniffing out opportunities like a truffle-hunting pig (minus the dirt and the snout).

Strategy 1: Stay Curious and Observant

Curiosity may have killed the cat, but in business, it's what brings fortunes to life. Many people move through the world on autopilot, content with routine and not questioning how things work or why they're done a certain way. But curiosity is the key to spotting gaps, inefficiencies, and overlooked ideas—the very things that pave the way for future Gold Rushes.

Take Jeff Bezos, for example. He didn't just wake up one day and think, "Hey, I'll sell books online." He was intensely curious about the internet and its potential for commerce, noticing that while most people were either skeptical or unaware of e-commerce's possibilities, the opportunity was wide open. That curiosity led to Amazon, and the rest, as they say, is history.

Exercise: The Curiosity Journal

- Start a "Curiosity Journal." Write down three things every day that you're curious about or that catch your attention. They don't have to be business-related. The idea is to train your brain to notice things that others overlook.
- Then, take a moment to brainstorm potential business implications for each. Even if most of them lead nowhere, you're practicing the art of noticing.

Strategy 2: Study and Track Micro-Trends

Gold Rushes don't appear out of thin air—they evolve from small shifts, or "micro-trends," that hint at broader changes. To the untrained eye, micro-trends are easy to miss or dismiss, but if you watch them closely, they often grow into large movements. By learning to spot these micro-trends early, you're setting yourself up to see the bigger picture before it becomes obvious.

Think about the organic food movement. Twenty years ago, the organic aisle in the grocery store was a niche, mostly unnoticed by the masses. But those who paid attention to growing consumer concerns about food quality and environmental impact realized that "organic" wasn't just a fad—it was a trend that would explode. And explode it did. Today, organic products are everywhere, and the early adopters who bet on it are reaping the rewards.

Exercise: Trend Radar

- Identify three micro-trends in any industry (fashion, technology, health, etc.). These can be things you've noticed or heard about, like a new app, a social media platform gaining traction, or a shift in consumer be-

havior.
- For each micro-trend, write down where it is now and where it could logically lead in the future. Challenge yourself to envision two to three potential outcomes or business ideas.
- Finally, rate each trend on a scale from 1 to 10 in terms of potential impact and likelihood of growth. This will help you prioritize which trends to watch more closely.

Strategy 3: Listen to the "Outliers" and Early Adopters

The trendsetters, the "outliers," and the early adopters are always the ones who drive new markets. They're the people trying new things, testing the edges of convention, and seeing possibilities where others see risks. If you want to predict emerging markets, spend time observing these groups and listening to their chatter. They're often the first to spot what's coming, because they're actively seeking change, not waiting for it.

One of the best examples? Social media influencers. A few years ago, most people dismissed the idea that someone could make a living from posting pictures or videos online. But early adopters saw the potential, and today, influencer marketing is a multi-billion-dollar industry.

Exercise: Outlier Analysis

- Identify three individuals, brands, or social media accounts known for pushing boundaries in a specific field.
- Spend time observing their content and noticing any recurring themes, products, or ideas they seem excited about. What new platforms, tools, or brands are they using?
- Take notes on any ideas that pop up from their posts. Pay attention to comments and discussions—they're often full of insights about what's resonating (or not) with their audience.

Strategy 4: Follow the Money Flow

In every Gold Rush, there are key financial indicators that suggest a market is heating up. In today's digital world, you can often get a feel for what's about to take off simply by tracking investments, acquisitions, and emerging companies. Venture capital firms, angel investors, and big companies are usually ahead of the curve, pouring money into technologies and markets they believe will boom.

For example, the rise of electric vehicles (EVs) was heavily backed by government incentives, venture capital, and major auto companies well before they hit the mainstream. Those who watched the flow of investments knew something big was on the horizon long before EVs became popular.

Exercise: Financial Pulse Check

- Subscribe to a financial news site or investment newsletter that tracks venture capital funding, IPOs, and acquisitions (e.g., Crunchbase, CB Insights).
- Identify three industries that are receiving significant investment or M&A (mergers and acquisitions) activity. For each, try to understand *why* this industry is seeing attention.
- Write down any companies that are new or in the spotlight, then dig into what they do, why they're interesting, and what problem they're solving.

Strategy 5: Pay Attention to Technological Advancements

Technology is a massive driver of new markets and Gold Rushes. Whenever a new technology emerges, it creates ripple effects that extend far beyond the original product. Just think of the smartphone: it didn't just create a new way to make phone calls; it launched entire industries from app development to mobile accessories. By keeping an eye on technological advancements, you can often get a front-row seat to what's about to change the game.

An example of this is artificial intelligence (AI). While AI has been in development for decades, recent advancements have moved it from sci-fi to practical application, impacting industries from finance to healthcare to entertainment. Those who recognized its potential early are leading the way in an entirely new market.

Exercise: Tech Radar

- Pick a specific area of technology that interests you (AI, biotech, renewable energy, etc.).
- Every week, set aside a few minutes to read up on recent advancements in that area, noting any new products, companies, or applications.
- As you read, look for signs of where the technology could be applied next. For example, if you read about a new AI algorithm for image recognition, think about where else it could be used (retail, manufacturing, healthcare, etc.).

Strategy 6: Monitor Social Shifts and Consumer Behavior

People don't just buy products; they buy solutions to problems, big and small. Shifts in social attitudes and consumer behavior often point to the next big thing. When people change how they live, what they prioritize, or what they care about, entire industries often spring up to meet these new needs.

Take wellness and mental health, for example. A decade ago, mental health was largely stigmatized. Today, it's a multi-billion-dollar industry, with products and services like meditation apps, wellness retreats, and mental health coaching seeing massive growth. Why? Because society shifted, and businesses evolved to meet the new demand.

Exercise: Behavioral Trend Map

- Identify two to three social shifts you've noticed in recent years (e.g., emphasis on sustainability, remote work culture, self-care, etc.).
- For each, brainstorm a list of industries or business

- ideas that could benefit from these changes.
- Choose one idea and map out the possible ways it could evolve over time. For example, if remote work continues to grow, consider the ripple effects on industries like coworking spaces, virtual team-building, and productivity tools.

Bringing It All Together: Your Gold Rush Toolkit

These exercises and strategies may seem simple, but don't underestimate their power. The goal is to hone your intuition, training yourself to see potential in the unexpected and develop a radar for spotting opportunity. And here's a final tip: **trust your instincts.** Predicting emerging markets isn't about following the crowd; it's about stepping back and seeing patterns where others don't.

Final Thoughts on Seeing Around Corners

Predicting the future is never foolproof, and there will always be risks involved. But with these strategies in your toolkit, you'll be better equipped to make educated, informed bets on what's coming next. And remember: even if a trend doesn't turn into the next Gold Rush, the skills you build here are invaluable. You're learning how to spot opportunities, analyze trends, and understand markets—all critical abilities for navigating the unpredictable world of entrepreneurship.

So, as you look around and see change unfolding in countless industries, start asking yourself: *What's around the corner?* The answer just might be the next big Gold Rush.

Part II: Getting Ready for the Gold Rush

CHAPTER 4: THE IMPORTANCE OF MINDSET AND RESILIENCE

Welcome to the not-so-glamorous but absolutely critical part of chasing a Gold Rush: resilience. You see, for every pioneering entrepreneur who hits it big, there are at least a dozen skeptics ready to call them crazy, irresponsible, or doomed to fail. If you're planning on spotting the next Gold Rush, you need to have something stronger than good ideas or funding—you need a mindset that stands its ground when others try to pull you off course. In other words, you need resilience.

Mindset isn't about positive affirmations or motivational posters; it's about building an inner fortress that protects your vision from naysayers and self-doubt. It's about believing in your idea so deeply that you're willing to hold on even when others are telling you to "play it safe" or "be realistic." In this chapter, we're going to dive into how to build that kind of mindset, with some help from entrepreneurs who stared skepticism in the face and came out stronger.

Building Confidence in Unconventional Ideas

Let's get one thing straight: unconventional ideas are rarely met with applause. When you propose a big, bold, or unusual concept, you're likely to be met with skepticism or outright criticism. Why? Because it's human nature to resist change. People prefer what's comfortable, predictable, and proven. When you show up with an idea that challenges the status quo, it makes people uncomfortable. And sometimes, that discomfort leads to doubt, discouragement, and maybe even a few eye-rolls.

Take Steve Jobs, for example. When Jobs first presented the idea of the iPhone, people told him it was absurd. Who needed a phone without buttons? Why would anyone want a device that's part phone, part internet browser, part music player? Even Apple's own engineers were skeptical. But Jobs had a vision, and he stuck to it. Today, the iPhone is one of the most successful products in history, and the world is a different place because one man dared to believe in his unconventional idea.

Lesson Learned: Confidence isn't about convincing others to believe in your idea. It's about having enough conviction in yourself that you don't need their approval. When you're building something bold, expect resistance—but don't let it shake you. Instead, let it fuel you.

Strategy 1: Developing a Resilient Mindset

Resilience isn't just a personality trait; it's a skill you can develop. It's about learning how to handle setbacks, criticism, and uncertainty without letting it erode your determination. Here are a few strategies for cultivating resilience:

1. **Reframe Setbacks as Learning Opportunities**: Every failure, setback, or criticism contains a lesson if you're willing to look for it. Instead of seeing setbacks as reasons to give up, view them as stepping stones. Many of the greatest breakthroughs happen because someone failed, learned, and came back stronger.
2. **Focus on Your "Why"**: When doubt creeps in, remem-

ber why you started in the first place. Your "why" should be something so powerful that it keeps you going even when things get tough. For Jobs, his "why" was about creating technology that changed people's lives. For Elon Musk, it's about building a sustainable future. When you have a strong "why," the "how" becomes much easier.

3. **Practice Self-Belief Every Day**: It sounds simple, but believing in yourself is a daily habit. Surround yourself with positive reinforcement, people who support your vision, and reminders of your own achievements. Self-belief isn't a switch you turn on once; it's a muscle you build every day.

Exercise: The Resilience Journal

- Every day, write down one thing you did that pushed you out of your comfort zone, one thing you learned from a setback, and one reason you believe in your idea. Over time, this journal will become a record of your growth, proof of your resilience, and a resource for when doubt inevitably creeps in.

Case Study: The Wright Brothers—Flying in the Face of Doubt

Let's talk about two brothers who faced not just skepticism, but ridicule. Orville and Wilbur Wright had a crazy dream: to build a machine that could fly. In the early 1900s, the idea of human flight was considered ridiculous, something only found in fairytales. The Wright brothers didn't have government grants or massive funding. They were bicycle mechanics, working out of a small shop, teaching themselves the principles of flight with trial, error, and grit.

People mocked them. Newspapers called them foolish. Experts said it couldn't be done. But they pressed on, experimenting with different designs, engines, and wing shapes. Finally, on December 17, 1903, the Wright brothers flew the first powered, controlled airplane in Kitty Hawk, North Carolina. And just like that, they rewrote history.

Lesson Learned: The Wright brothers succeeded not because they had unlimited resources or expert knowledge but because they had resilience. They kept going when the world told them to stop, and their persistence changed the course of history.

Mindset Tip: Surround yourself with stories like these. When the going gets tough, remember that history is filled with people who were doubted, ridiculed, and told to give up—only to succeed beyond everyone's expectations.

Strategy 2: Embrace the Power of a Growth Mindset

A growth mindset is the belief that abilities and intelligence can be developed through effort, learning, and perseverance. Instead of seeing setbacks as a sign of failure, people with a growth mindset see them as opportunities to grow and improve. Adopting this mindset makes you more resilient because it shifts your focus from avoiding failure to embracing growth.

Take Oprah Winfrey as an example. Today, she's an icon, but she didn't get there without facing her fair share of challenges. In her early career, she was told she didn't have the right "look" to be on television. She was even fired from her first news anchor job. But Oprah didn't let that stop her. She continued to develop her skills, refine her craft, and learn from each setback. Her growth mindset turned her into one of the most influential people in the world.

Mindset Tip: The next time you're faced with criticism, ask yourself, "What can I learn from this?" Instead of letting it discourage you, use it as a stepping stone. Developing a growth mindset means you're always moving forward, no matter the obstacles.

Case Study: Sara Blakely—Turning Rejection into Resilience

If anyone knows about resilience, it's Sara Blakely, the founder of

Spanx. Long before she became the world's youngest self-made female billionaire, Blakely was working a job she didn't love and constantly facing rejection. In fact, she tried to become a lawyer but failed the LSAT twice. When she had the idea for Spanx—a comfortable, slimming undergarment for women—she pitched it to numerous manufacturers and investors. Almost all of them turned her down.

But Blakely didn't let the rejection stop her. She used it as fuel. She believed so strongly in her idea that she kept going, even when people laughed at her and told her no one would buy her product. She worked tirelessly to bring Spanx to market, and eventually, her persistence paid off. Today, Spanx is a billion-dollar brand, and Blakely's story is a testament to the power of resilience.

Lesson Learned: Rejection is part of the journey, not a reason to quit. Blakely faced setback after setback, but she didn't let it shake her confidence. She learned from each "no" and kept pushing forward.

Mindset Tip: When faced with rejection, ask yourself, "What can I do differently next time?" Use each rejection as feedback, adjust your approach, and keep moving forward. Each "no" is one step closer to a "yes."

Strategy 3: Build a Supportive Network

Resilience doesn't mean you have to go it alone. Surrounding yourself with a supportive network can make all the difference when the going gets tough. Your network doesn't need to be huge—it just needs to be filled with people who believe in you, challenge you to keep going, and remind you why you started in the first place.

In fact, many entrepreneurs attribute their resilience to the people around them. Elon Musk, who has faced criticism and skepticism throughout his career, relies on a close circle of advisors, colleagues, and friends who understand his vision and encourage him to keep going. Building that kind of network is crucial for anyone pursuing big dreams.

Exercise: Identify Your Support System

- Make a list of people who encourage and support you. This could be family, friends, mentors, or even online communities.
- Identify at least one person you can go to when you're feeling discouraged or doubtful. Having someone to talk to can help you regain perspective and keep pushing forward.
- If you don't have a strong support system yet, start building one. Join industry groups, networking events, or online communities where people share your interests and understand your journey.

Strategy 4: Embrace Patience and Long-Term Thinking

In a world obsessed with instant gratification, patience is one of the most underrated qualities of successful entrepreneurs. Real success doesn't happen overnight—it's the result of years of hard work, learning, and persistence. Embracing a long-term mindset will help you stay resilient through the ups and downs of your journey.

Consider Warren Buffett, one of the most successful investors of all time. Buffett didn't build his wealth by chasing quick wins; he invested with a long-term view. He famously said, "The stock market is a device for transferring money from the impatient to the patient." The same is true for entrepreneurship. If you're in it for the long haul, setbacks become temporary hurdles, not roadblocks.

Mindset Tip: Practice thinking long-term. When you're feeling discouraged, remind yourself that great things take time. Building something worthwhile is a marathon, not a sprint.

Final Thoughts on Building a Resilient Mindset

If you're serious about chasing Gold Rush opportunities, resilience isn't optional—it's essential. You're going to encounter skeptics, setbacks, and moments of self-doubt. But with the right mindset, you'll be able to weather the storm, hold your ground, and push through where others give up.

Remember, resilience isn't about never facing challenges; it's about learning to face them with strength, confidence, and a refusal to quit. Every "no" brings you closer to a "yes," every setback is a setup for a comeback, and every doubter is just one more reason to succeed. So build that inner fortress, believe in your vision, and keep pushing forward. The next Gold Rush is waiting—you just have to be resilient enough to claim it.

CHAPTER 5: DEVELOPING A UNIQUE VALUE PROPOSITION

You've got resilience. You've got vision. Now it's time to create something that others can't resist—something so compelling that when people see it, they think, *Where have you been all my life?* That's the magic of a unique value proposition (UVP), and it's essential for standing out in a Gold Rush market.

Think of your UVP as the hook that catches people's attention and keeps them coming back. It's not just about having a good product or service; it's about offering something so distinct, so valuable, that it becomes the only logical choice. In this chapter, we'll dive into the process of creating a UVP that isn't just unique—it's irresistible.

The Power of Solving Unaddressed Needs

Before you can develop a UVP, you need to understand what it's meant to do: meet an unaddressed need. A Gold Rush market is full of opportunity, but that also means it's often full of people offering similar products or services. To cut through the noise, your UVP has to go beyond the basics. It has to address a specific need or pain point that others are overlooking.

Let's look at an example that changed the way we think about taxis: Uber. Before Uber, the taxi industry was, well, stagnant. Getting a ride meant hailing a cab on the street, calling a dispatcher, or relying on inconsistent service. Uber identified an unaddressed need—people wanted a faster, easier, and more reliable way to get around—and created a service that met it. Their UVP? "Get a ride at the touch of a button." Simple, effective, and exactly what people wanted.

Lesson Learned: The best UVPs solve a specific problem that competitors haven't addressed. When you can identify a pain point and solve it in a unique way, you're already on the path to creating an irresistible offer.

Step 1: Identifying Your Market's Pain Points

The first step in developing a UVP is understanding the problems your target market faces. Gold Rush markets, especially, have lots of unmet needs because they're new, evolving, and often lacking fully established solutions. By diving deep into the pain points your potential customers experience, you can position yourself as the answer to their problems.

Exercise: Pain Point Mapping

- List out the biggest frustrations, challenges, and unmet needs your potential customers might face. These could be practical issues (e.g., lack of convenience) or emotional pain points (e.g., lack of trust or reliability).
- Group similar pain points together, and look for patterns. These patterns reveal key areas where existing solutions fall short.
- Ask yourself: *What can I offer that will make these pain points disappear?* The answer to that question will guide your UVP.

Case Study: Dollar Shave Club—A Simple Solution to a Common

Problem

Before Dollar Shave Club entered the market, buying razors was a pretty painful experience. You'd have to go to a store, deal with high prices, and often end up with more razors than you needed. Dollar Shave Club's founders saw an opportunity to solve these pain points by offering a simple solution: quality razors delivered to your door for a low price. Their UVP? "A great shave for a few bucks a month." Simple, relatable, and effective.

By focusing on an unaddressed need (affordable, convenient shaving), they were able to cut through the noise and appeal directly to people's frustrations. Dollar Shave Club's success shows that you don't have to reinvent the wheel—you just have to make it spin a little smoother.

Lesson Learned: The most effective UVPs don't overcomplicate things. They solve a problem in a way that's easy for people to understand and appreciate.

Step 2: Crafting a Clear and Compelling UVP

Once you've identified the pain points, it's time to craft your UVP. This is the message that tells your customers *why* they should choose you over everyone else. It should be clear, concise, and compelling enough to stick in people's minds.

A good UVP has three main components:

1. **Specificity**: What exactly do you offer, and what makes it valuable? Don't try to appeal to everyone. Be specific about who your product is for and what it does.
2. **Differentiation**: Why should customers choose you over the competition? What sets you apart? If you're doing something unique, make it obvious.
3. **Benefit**: How does your product improve the customer's life? Focus on the outcome or solution your

product provides, rather than just its features.

Formula for a UVP: [Product/Service] helps [Target Audience] solve [Problem] by providing [Unique Solution]. Here's an example: "Uber helps people get a reliable ride quickly by offering on-demand, app-based car service."

Exercise: UVP Workshop

- Write down a draft of your UVP using the formula above.
- Simplify it to one sentence. Don't worry about making it perfect; just focus on clarity.
- Share it with friends, colleagues, or potential customers, and ask if it's clear, specific, and compelling. Revise based on their feedback until it's razor-sharp.

Case Study: Airbnb—More Than Just a Place to Stay

When Airbnb launched, the concept was almost laughable. Stay in a stranger's home? Pay for an air mattress in someone's living room? Yet, Airbnb's founders saw a powerful need: travelers wanted affordable, unique places to stay, and homeowners had extra space they could rent out. Airbnb's UVP? "Belong Anywhere."

This simple message tapped into the universal desire for connection, exploration, and affordability. It wasn't just about offering a room—it was about creating an experience. Today, Airbnb is a household name, and their UVP has helped transform the travel industry.

Lesson Learned: An irresistible UVP goes beyond functional benefits. It taps into something emotional or experiential that makes customers feel a connection to the brand.

Step 3: Make Your Offering Irresistible

An irresistible offer isn't just about the product itself—it's about how you position, package, and present it. The best UVPs create a sense of urgency, exclusivity, or must-have appeal that makes customers feel like they can't pass it up. This might involve bundling services, offering a limited-time deal, or highlighting unique aspects that competitors can't easily replicate.

Strategies for Making Your Offer Irresistible:

1. **Add Scarcity or Urgency**: People don't want to miss out. Limited-time offers, exclusive memberships, or limited-edition products make your offering feel more desirable.
2. **Create a Sense of Belonging**: Brands like Harley-Davidson and CrossFit don't just offer products; they offer community. Customers feel like they're part of something bigger, which creates loyalty and repeat business.
3. **Emphasize the Benefit, Not Just the Feature**: Features are great, but benefits are what people care about. For example, if you sell noise-canceling headphones, focus on the benefit ("Experience pure, undisturbed focus") rather than just the feature ("Noise-canceling technology").

Exercise: The "Must-Have" Test

- Ask yourself, *What makes this product a must-have instead of a nice-to-have?* Write down the answers.
- Then, brainstorm ways to amplify those aspects. Could you make it exclusive? Could you offer a special bonus? How can you make customers feel that they *need* what you're offering, not just want it?

Case Study: Tesla—The Allure of Exclusivity and Innovation

Tesla didn't just enter the automotive market; it created an entirely new category. When Tesla launched, electric vehicles were seen as niche, environmentally friendly, but impractical. Tesla's UVP wasn't just about being electric—it was about luxury, performance, and innovation. They created a sense of exclusivity and made people feel like owning a Tesla was more than just owning a car—it was a status symbol.

Tesla's UVP isn't just about eco-friendliness; it's about experiencing the future. And with every innovation, Tesla reinforces this UVP by pushing the boundaries of what people expect from a car. The result? Tesla owners aren't just customers—they're advocates.

Lesson Learned: When developing a UVP, think about how you can make your product feel exclusive, innovative, or forward-thinking. Tesla succeeded by turning an ordinary concept (electric vehicles) into an extraordinary experience.

Step 4: Testing and Refining Your UVP

Once you've crafted your UVP, the work doesn't stop there. A good UVP is always evolving based on customer feedback, market changes, and your own growth. Testing and refining your UVP ensures it stays relevant and compelling, especially as the market becomes more competitive.

Strategies for Testing Your UVP:

1. **Get Feedback from Real Customers**: Conduct interviews or surveys to see how your target audience responds to your UVP. Are they excited? Confused? Underwhelmed?
2. **A/B Testing**: If you're marketing online, A/B testing different versions of your UVP can help you see which one resonates most.
3. **Iterate Based on Results**: Don't be afraid to make tweaks based on what you learn. Your UVP should grow with your brand, not remain static.

Exercise: UVP Audit

- Every few months, take a fresh look at your UVP. Ask yourself if it still aligns with your customers' needs, differentiates you from competitors, and captures the essence of your brand.
- If not, make adjustments. The more you refine, the sharper your UVP becomes.

Final Thoughts on Crafting a Winning UVP

A UVP is more than just a clever tagline—it's the essence of your business. It's what makes customers choose you over others, what keeps them coming back, and what turns a product into a brand. In a Gold Rush market, where competition is fierce and opportunities are fleeting, your UVP is your ticket to standing out and winning over customers.

The best UVPs solve real problems, address unmet needs, and create something people can't resist. So take the time to develop yours, test it, refine it, and make sure it's something that speaks to your target audience on a deep level. Because when you get your UVP right, it's not just a statement—it's a promise.

CHAPTER 6: BUILDING NETWORKS AND RESOURCES

Imagine for a moment that you've spotted an incredible opportunity in an emerging market. You have the vision, the product, and the plan. Now, all you need are the resources and connections to turn that vision into reality. And here's the truth: no matter how brilliant your idea is, you can't do it alone. Even the most successful entrepreneurs needed a network of allies, mentors, investors, and strategic partners to help them along the way.

Building a powerful network is one of the most valuable investments you can make, especially when diving into new, uncharted territory. It's like assembling a team of expert guides who can help you navigate the mountains and valleys of a Gold Rush market. This chapter will walk you through the essentials of networking, from finding mentors and industry insiders to attracting investors and forming strategic partnerships. Because in the world of business, who you know can be as important as what you know.

Why Connections Matter in a Gold Rush Market

A Gold Rush market moves fast. Competition is fierce, information changes rapidly, and new trends emerge seemingly overnight. In this environment, having the right connections is like having a front-row seat to the action. Your network can open doors to insider knowledge, new opportunities, and valuable resources, all of which can give you a competitive edge.

Consider Airbnb's rise to fame. Founders Brian Chesky and Joe Gebbia weren't just trying to build a business—they were trying to disrupt an entire industry. To do that, they needed investors who believed in their vision and mentors who could guide them. With the help of connections through the startup accelerator Y Combinator, they gained access to mentorship, funding, and connections with key players in Silicon Valley. Those early connections were instrumental in Airbnb's rapid growth.

Lesson Learned: Building a network isn't just about meeting people—it's about creating a support system that can provide insights, resources, and access to new opportunities. In a Gold Rush market, your network is your lifeline.

Step 1: Finding the Right Mentors

A good mentor is like a compass in uncharted territory. They've been through the ups and downs, they know the industry landscape, and they can help you avoid pitfalls while guiding you toward success. But finding the right mentor isn't as simple as sending a LinkedIn message—it's about building genuine relationships with people who understand your goals and can offer valuable guidance.

Tips for Finding a Mentor:

1. **Be Clear About What You Need**: Not every mentor is the right fit. Some may specialize in strategy, while others are experts in funding or scaling. Know what you need from a mentor and seek out someone who excels in that area.
2. **Look for Industry Leaders and Pioneers**: Seek out people who have succeeded in or have deep knowledge of your target market. Whether they're CEOs, thought leaders, or retired executives, these are people who can

offer high-level guidance and a wealth of experience.
3. **Engage in Their Sphere**: Don't just reach out out of the blue. Attend their speaking events, join industry groups they're involved in, or engage with them on social media. Building rapport over time creates a foundation for a more natural, long-lasting relationship.

Exercise: Mentor Wishlist

- Write down a list of qualities and expertise you'd like in a mentor. Then, identify 3–5 people who fit the bill and research ways to engage with them.
- Attend an event where they're speaking, comment on their posts, or reach out with a thoughtful message about their work. Remember, mentorship is a two-way street—approach it with genuine interest and respect.

Case Study: Eric Schmidt and Google Founders

When Google was just starting, founders Larry Page and Sergey Brin were brilliant innovators but new to the intricacies of running a large business. They sought out a mentor who could help them scale without losing their vision. They found that mentor in Eric Schmidt, who later became Google's CEO. Schmidt's guidance helped transform Google from a startup into a tech powerhouse.

Lesson Learned: A good mentor can offer perspectives you might miss and help you navigate the complexities of growth. Seek out mentors who align with your goals and can provide strategic insights at key stages in your journey.

Step 2: Building Industry Connections

Networking within your industry is about more than just collecting business cards. It's about building relationships that can provide market insights, keep you updated on trends, and connect you with potential collaborators. In a Gold Rush market, staying informed is crucial, and the best information often comes from insiders.

Strategies for Building Industry Connections:

1. **Join Industry Groups and Associations**: Almost every industry has professional groups or associations. These organizations offer networking events, online forums, and other resources that can connect you with key players in your field.
2. **Attend Conferences and Trade Shows**: Industry events are prime networking opportunities. Not only do you meet potential collaborators, but you also gain insight into what's happening on the front lines of your industry.
3. **Network Digitally**: LinkedIn, Twitter, and industry-specific forums are great places to connect with people. Don't just focus on people at the top—sometimes, connections with peers can be just as valuable, especially if they're moving into the same space.

Exercise: Targeted Networking Plan

- Identify one or two key industry groups or events you could join or attend within the next three months.
- Set a goal to connect with at least five people from these groups. Don't aim to make every conversation transactional; focus on genuinely learning from them and finding ways to offer value in return.

Case Study: Steve Jobs and the Silicon Valley Network

Steve Jobs knew the value of industry connections from the beginning. Even before Apple became a household name, Jobs was networking with key players in Silicon Valley. He built relationships with other tech founders, venture capitalists, and engineers, which gave him access to talent, funding, and support at critical stages.

Lesson Learned: Surround yourself with people who share your ambitions and who can help you stay informed and inspired. Jobs didn't just build a network; he built a support system that played a role in Apple's success.

Step 3: Attracting Investors and Capital

In a Gold Rush market, access to capital can be the difference between seizing an opportunity and watching it slip away. While bootstrapping is possible, having investors on board can help you scale faster, especially if they bring more than just funding to the table. The key is attracting investors who believe in your vision and can offer strategic value.

Tips for Attracting Investors:

1. **Research Investor Profiles**: Not all investors are alike. Some specialize in specific industries, while others look for early-stage companies. Research potential investors to find those who align with your market and growth stage.
2. **Develop a Compelling Pitch**: Investors want to see a clear path to profitability and growth. Craft a pitch that outlines your unique value proposition, market potential, and plan for scaling. Be specific about how their investment will fuel growth.
3. **Show Traction**: Investors love proof. Demonstrating traction, whether it's through early sales, partnerships, or user engagement, can make your pitch far more compelling.

Exercise: Investor Profile List

- Create a list of potential investors, noting their interests, recent investments, and any connections you might have with them.
- Tailor your pitch to each investor, highlighting aspects

of your business that align with their investment style and priorities.

Case Study: Netflix and the Power of Venture Capital

Netflix's journey from DVD rentals to streaming giant wasn't funded by revenue alone. Early investors saw the potential in Reed Hastings' vision and backed the company through its rapid scaling. Netflix's investors didn't just provide funds—they provided support, mentorship, and introductions that helped the company transform the entertainment industry.

Lesson Learned: Investors are more than just funders—they're partners who can open doors, offer insights, and provide the capital needed to pursue opportunities at scale. Look for investors who align with your goals and can help you grow strategically.

Step 4: Forming Strategic Partnerships

In emerging markets, strategic partnerships can provide you with resources, visibility, and access that would be difficult to obtain alone. The right partner can help you tap into new customer bases, increase credibility, or provide operational support.

Tips for Finding Strategic Partners:

1. **Identify Complementary Businesses**: Look for companies that serve the same audience but aren't direct competitors. Partnerships work best when each party brings something unique to the table.
2. **Align on Goals and Values**: A partnership is like a business marriage. Ensure your potential partner shares your values and goals for the collaboration to be mutually beneficial.
3. **Define Roles and Responsibilities**: Be clear about who will handle what and set expectations from the start. A well-defined partnership runs smoothly and avoids potential conflicts down the line.

Exercise: Strategic Partner Brainstorm

- Make a list of potential partners that serve a similar audience but offer a different product or service.
- Reach out to gauge their interest in collaborating. Start small with a co-marketing campaign or a joint event to test the waters.

Case Study: Apple and Nike—A Strategic Alliance in Wearable Tech

When Apple introduced the Apple Watch, they wanted it to be more than just a gadget—they wanted it to be a fitness and lifestyle device. To make that vision a reality, they partnered with Nike, a brand with deep expertise in fitness and lifestyle products. Together, they created the Apple Watch Nike+, blending Apple's tech with Nike's fitness expertise.

Lesson Learned: Strategic partnerships can elevate your brand, extend your reach, and provide expertise that complements your own. In the right partnership, both companies benefit from shared resources, insights, and audiences.

Final Thoughts on Networking and Building Resources

In a Gold Rush market, the right connections can be the difference between success and stagnation. Whether it's a mentor to guide you, an industry insider to keep you informed, an investor to fund your growth, or a partner to amplify your impact, building a network of allies is essential for long-term success.

But remember, networking isn't about using people or quick gains—it's about building genuine, mutually beneficial relationships that provide value over time. Approach each connection with respect, curiosity, and a willingness to offer value in return. Because in the end, a strong network is a powerful resource that can help you achieve your vision and navigate the ups and downs of any

Gold Rush market.

Part III: Leveraging the Opportunity

CHAPTER 7: THE FIRST-MOVER ADVANTAGE AND ITS RISKS

Let's talk about one of the most enticing concepts in the world of business: the first-mover advantage. It's the idea that by being first in a new market, you get a head start on everyone else. You're the first brand people hear about, the initial name associated with the product or service, and you're often able to build a loyal customer base before others even enter the game. But as exciting as this advantage is, being first comes with its fair share of risks. The trailblazer has to clear a path through uncharted territory, and sometimes, that means encountering unexpected challenges.

In this chapter, we'll explore the benefits and pitfalls of the first-mover advantage, look at real-world examples, and outline strategies for making sure your pioneering move doesn't leave you lost in the wilderness.

The Rewards of Being First

The first-mover advantage is all about capturing market share before anyone else gets a chance. When you're the first brand in a new space, people remember you. You set the standards, define customer expectations, and often build brand loyalty that makes it hard for others to compete. Here are some key benefits of being the first to enter a market:

1. **Reduced Competition**: By entering early, you're essentially carving out a niche with minimal competition. You don't have to fight for attention—you've already got it. Think of Netflix in the early days of streaming. With few competitors, they quickly became synonymous with online entertainment.
2. **Brand Establishment**: When you're first, you get to be the brand that defines the market. Just as Google became synonymous with search and Zoom became synonymous with video calls, a first mover has the chance to set the tone and become the go-to name in the industry.
3. **Building Customer Loyalty**: Early adopters are often highly loyal to the first brand they try, especially if it meets their needs. These loyal customers become brand advocates, spreading the word and creating organic growth that later entrants have to work much harder to achieve.
4. **Higher Pricing Power**: When you're first, you often have the luxury of setting prices without comparison. With no direct competition, you can establish pricing standards that others must follow, allowing you to maximize initial profits.

Exercise: First-Mover Opportunities

- Think of a market or trend you've noticed emerging. Imagine yourself as the first brand entering that space. What advantages would you have? Write down at least three ways being first could set you apart.

Case Study: Tesla—Pioneering the Electric Vehicle Market

Tesla's rise as a pioneer in electric vehicles is a classic example of the first-mover advantage. When Elon Musk's company began producing electric cars, the idea was met with skepticism. But by entering early, Tesla was able to establish itself as the leader in the electric vehicle space. Tesla didn't just create cars; they created a brand associated with luxury, innovation, and environmental consciousness.

The first-mover advantage allowed Tesla to build a passionate customer base, capture significant market share, and become the brand synonymous with electric vehicles. Today, other automakers are racing to catch up, but Tesla remains the industry leader, setting trends in design, technology, and even distribution with their direct-to-consumer model.

Lesson Learned: Being the first doesn't just mean entering early—it means setting the standard. Tesla's success shows that a pioneer who creates a compelling brand identity and strong customer loyalty can keep competitors at bay, even as the market becomes crowded.

The Risks of Being First

As tempting as the first-mover advantage is, pioneering a new market isn't without its risks. Being first means taking on challenges that others will be able to learn from and avoid. Here are some of the key risks that come with being an early entrant:

1. **High Costs of Market Education**: When you're the first, it's often up to you to educate the market about why they need your product or service. This can be costly and time-consuming. For example, when Airbnb first launched, they had to convince people that staying in a stranger's home was not only safe but preferable to traditional hotels. Convincing a skeptical audience is part of the first-mover challenge.
2. **Unproven Demand**: In a new market, demand can be unpredictable. You're betting that people will want

what you're offering, but there's no guarantee. If the market isn't ready, you risk investing time and money in something that won't gain traction.
3. **Technological and Operational Uncertainty**: Often, pioneers enter a market where the technology is still evolving or where there's no clear operational roadmap. This means facing bugs, inefficiencies, or technical barriers that later entrants can avoid once the groundwork is laid.
4. **Attracting Competitors**: Ironically, the success of a first mover often attracts competitors. Once others see a profitable market emerging, they jump in, benefiting from the groundwork laid by the pioneer. These competitors can learn from the pioneer's mistakes and improve upon their product, making it harder for the first mover to maintain dominance.

Exercise: Risk Assessment

- Think of a pioneering idea you're interested in pursuing. Write down three potential risks you'd face as a first mover and brainstorm ways to address each risk. Consider costs, market readiness, and potential technological challenges.

Case Study: Friendster—The Social Network That Was Too Early

Before Facebook, there was Friendster, one of the first social networking sites. Launched in 2002, Friendster quickly became popular, but it faced significant challenges. The site was plagued with slow load times, technical issues, and struggled to scale as its user base grew. In contrast, Facebook entered the social media landscape a few years later with better technology, a clear business model, and the advantage of learning from Friendster's missteps.

Friendster's early entrance into the social media space attracted a lot of interest, but its inability to keep up with demand and its technological struggles eventually led to its decline. Facebook, as a fast follower, was able to capture the market Friendster pioneered and eventually became the world's dominant social network.

Lesson Learned: The first-mover advantage isn't a guarantee of success. If a pioneer can't keep up with growth or address foundational issues, fast followers can come in and dominate the space. Friendster's downfall reminds us that being first requires a commitment to adaptability and scalability.

Strategies for Managing First-Mover Risks

So how do you balance the benefits of pioneering with the risks? It comes down to being prepared, adaptable, and proactive. Here are some strategies to help you navigate the challenges of uncharted territory.

1. **Start Small and Test the Market**: Before going all in, start with a small, manageable launch to test demand. This allows you to validate your product or service with early adopters without overcommitting resources. You'll gain feedback, identify issues, and adjust as needed.
2. **Invest in Market Education**: If your product or service is truly new, invest in educating your target audience. This might mean creating informative content, running ad campaigns, or even partnering with influencers who can help promote your product. The goal is to build trust and show people why they need what you're offering.
3. **Focus on Quality and Reliability**: When you're the first in a market, reputation matters. People are skeptical of new products, and if you encounter issues, they're likely to remember them. Invest in quality control, reliable customer service, and user-friendly de-

sign to ensure a positive experience for early adopters.
4. **Stay Agile and Adaptive**: As a pioneer, you need to be ready to pivot if the market changes or new information emerges. Early adopters are a valuable source of feedback, and they'll let you know what works and what doesn't. Embrace their insights, and be willing to adapt your approach if necessary.
5. **Build a Strong Brand Identity**: When competitors inevitably enter the market, your brand identity can be your biggest defense. Build a brand that resonates with people on an emotional level. Companies like Apple and Tesla didn't just offer products—they offered visions of the future. A strong brand can create customer loyalty that's difficult for newcomers to replicate.

Exercise: Risk Mitigation Plan

- Identify a pioneering idea or product you're interested in. For each of the strategies above, write down a specific action you could take to mitigate risks as a first mover. This could include ideas for market testing, brand-building strategies, or ways to stay agile in response to feedback.

Case Study: Amazon—Mastering the First-Mover Advantage with Adaptability

Amazon didn't start as the e-commerce giant it is today. When Jeff Bezos founded the company, it was an online bookstore, a concept that seemed niche at the time. But Bezos had a clear vision: he wanted Amazon to become the "Everything Store." Amazon's initial success with books gave them the confidence and funding to expand into other categories.

What set Amazon apart was its adaptability. Bezos reinvested profits into developing a world-class distribution network, innovating with features like one-click ordering, and constantly refining Amazon's offerings. While other companies tried to enter e-commerce, Amazon's relentless focus on customer experience and long-term adaptability allowed it to maintain its lead, turning a first-mover advantage into lasting dominance.

Lesson Learned: Amazon's story illustrates that the key to maintaining a first-mover advantage is adaptability. The company didn't just rely on being first; it continued to innovate, improve, and grow, ultimately becoming the leader in e-commerce.

Final Thoughts on the First-Mover Advantage

Being first in a market is thrilling, but it's not for the faint of heart. The rewards of pioneering are immense—brand establishment, loyal customers, and industry recognition. But the challenges are equally real, from high costs to the constant threat of fast-following competitors. Success as a first mover requires a balanced approach: embracing the benefits of early entry while staying vigilant and adaptable to manage the risks.

Remember, being first isn't just about having a good idea—it's about executing it in a way that builds lasting value. So, as you embark on your own journey into uncharted territory, make sure you're prepared to handle the challenges, ready to adapt, and determined to make your mark. Because the only thing better than being first in a Gold Rush market is staying first.

CHAPTER 8: THE POWER OF SUPPORTING INDUSTRIES

If the Gold Rush taught us one thing, it's this: the ones who struck it richest weren't always the ones mining for gold. While many rushed to California in hopes of finding fortune, others saw an entirely different opportunity. Instead of seeking gold, they focused on supplying the dreamers and the diggers—the people who actually needed tools, gear, food, and shelter to chase their goals. These "supporting" entrepreneurs quietly built fortunes by meeting the essential needs of the market.

This strategy of succeeding through support remains powerful today. When a new industry or trend begins to surge, it creates an ecosystem of demand for tools, resources, and infrastructure that allow it to thrive. By identifying these gaps and fulfilling those needs, you can achieve success without necessarily taking on the risks of direct competition. In this chapter, we'll dive into the power of supporting industries, using case studies to highlight their impact and strategies for spotting demand gaps around major trends.

The Golden Shovel Opportunity

During the California Gold Rush, miners weren't the only ones making money. Savvy entrepreneurs who provided supplies to miners often ended up wealthier than the miners themselves. They sold shovels, picks, pans, food, clothing, and even entertainment. Demand was so high, and competition so low, that these suppliers were able to charge high prices, creating enormous profit margins.

One of the most famous examples is Levi Strauss. While Strauss didn't strike gold, he struck something perhaps even more valuable: the opportunity to supply durable work pants to miners. Strauss created a new product—denim jeans—that met the needs of hardworking miners. His "shovels" weren't literal tools, but they were indispensable to those digging for gold. Today, Levi's is a household name, thanks to a man who saw a gap and filled it in a way that others hadn't.

Lesson Learned: Sometimes the real opportunity isn't in the "gold" itself but in supplying the tools and infrastructure needed by those chasing it. Supporting industries play a critical role in emerging markets and can yield success without the inherent risk of competing directly.

Case Study: Shopify—Providing Tools for the E-commerce Gold Rush

As e-commerce began to take off in the early 2000s, there was a growing need for businesses to establish online stores. While some businesses invested heavily in custom-built websites, others struggled with the technical demands and high costs. Enter Shopify. Shopify didn't attempt to compete with individual e-commerce stores; instead, they became the go-to platform for building and managing online shops.

Shopify's value lay in its simplicity, flexibility, and support. It provided the digital "shovels" that thousands of entrepreneurs needed to succeed in e-commerce, from tools for setting up storefronts to payment processing, inventory management, and analytics. By focusing on support, Shopify created a multi-billion-dollar business without competing directly with any online store.

Lesson Learned: Supporting industries thrive by offering accessible, reliable, and scalable solutions that meet essential needs. Shopify didn't join the e-commerce race—they enabled it. By providing infrastructure and support, they created a valuable niche that continues to grow alongside the e-commerce industry.

Spotting Gaps in Demand

The key to success in a supporting industry is recognizing where demand is underserved. When a trend or industry begins to grow, it creates new needs for tools, technologies, and resources. Spotting these demand gaps is often about paying attention to pain points and inefficiencies within the industry. Here are some tips to help you identify where you might find a "shovel" opportunity:

1. **Identify Repeated Problems**: Observe common complaints, challenges, or bottlenecks faced by participants in a growing market. If everyone in a new industry is talking about the difficulty of securing a certain resource or tool, that's a clear opportunity.
2. **Look for Infrastructure Needs**: New markets often require logistical and operational support to function. This could mean warehousing, distribution, digital infrastructure, or even compliance support if the industry is regulated. If the market lacks established infrastructure, consider whether you could fill the gap.
3. **Spot Technology Gaps**: In many emerging industries, technology is critical but still catching up to demand. For example, the rise of renewable energy created a need for better battery storage solutions. Identifying gaps in technology can help you provide tools that support the industry's growth.

4. **Watch for Necessary Education and Training**: When industries are new, people often need education or certification to participate effectively. Training programs, courses, or credentialing services can be an effective way to tap into growing demand.

Exercise: Demand Gap Analysis

- Identify an emerging industry you're interested in. List the top three problems you've heard people in that industry mention.
- For each problem, brainstorm at least one type of support service, product, or tool that could address the gap.
- Evaluate each option to see if it could form a potential "shovel" opportunity that meets an essential need.

Case Study: Slack—Supporting Remote Work

As remote work grew in popularity, so did the need for efficient, effective communication tools. Slack didn't just fill this gap—they created an entirely new category for workplace messaging that enabled distributed teams to stay connected. While Slack wasn't the first company to offer workplace communication, they were the first to create a platform that felt as natural as texting.

By focusing on the unique challenges of remote teams, Slack developed a "shovel" for the modern workforce. They helped remote workers and companies transition smoothly to a new work model by providing tools for streamlined communication and collaboration. Today, Slack is one of the leading tools in the business productivity space.

Lesson Learned: Slack's success underscores the importance of understanding your audience's unique needs. By focusing on the specific pain points of remote teams, they created a must-have tool that became indispensable in the remote work ecosystem.

The Benefits of Supporting Industries

While pioneers in an industry often get the glory, supporting industries enjoy several advantages that make them appealing from a business perspective. Here are a few reasons why the "shovel" approach is a smart way to enter an emerging market:

1. **Reduced Direct Competition**: Instead of competing with front-runners, you're supporting them. This allows you to carve out a niche without taking on the same level of competition as primary players in the industry.
2. **Lower Risk**: Supporting industries often face less uncertainty. By providing an essential tool or service, you're meeting a steady demand that doesn't rely on the market's speculative success.
3. **Stable Revenue Stream**: Supporting businesses, especially those providing critical infrastructure or tools, benefit from recurring demand. As long as the industry continues to grow, there will be a consistent need for supporting services.
4. **Early and Lasting Brand Loyalty**: Companies and individuals in new industries tend to stay loyal to the brands that help them get established. By becoming an early supporter, you can create long-lasting relationships with clients and build brand loyalty.

Exercise: Supporting Industry Brainstorm

- Pick an industry or trend that interests you. Write down three essential tools, services, or infrastructure components that you think would be needed for the industry to grow.
- Next to each, jot down how you could provide or improve upon this support.
- Consider whether any of these ideas could serve as a foundation for a business that supports the industry while avoiding direct competition.

Case Study: Airbnb Experiences—Expanding the Travel Ecosystem

Airbnb initially made waves by helping people rent out their homes to travelers. But once they had an established user base, they recognized an additional need: unique experiences for travelers who wanted more than just a place to stay. Enter Airbnb Experiences—a platform that connects travelers with locals who offer guided tours, workshops, and other immersive activities.

Airbnb didn't compete directly with tour companies; instead, they expanded their role as a supportive platform for travel-related services. By creating a marketplace for experiences, Airbnb gave local hosts a way to earn extra income while enhancing the travel experience for their customers.

Lesson Learned: Supporting industries don't have to be limited to infrastructure—they can also include adjacent services that complement the primary product. Airbnb recognized that they could expand their platform to offer additional value without competing directly in the tourism market, allowing them to serve as a one-stop-shop for travelers.

Practical Tips for Entering a Supporting Industry

So, how can you position yourself as a successful player in a supporting industry? Here are some practical steps to help you establish yourself as a go-to resource for companies in emerging markets:

1. **Research the Core Needs of the Industry**: Understanding what companies in an industry need to succeed is essential. Talk to industry players, read industry publications, and keep an eye on the pain points that seem to be common across the board.
2. **Identify Your Unique Contribution**: Look for a way to

add unique value. Perhaps you can create a tool that's faster, cheaper, or more user-friendly than existing options. Or maybe you can bundle services to offer a comprehensive solution that simplifies operations for other businesses.
3. **Build Partnerships**: In a supporting role, relationships are key. Forge partnerships with companies in the primary industry and position yourself as an ally in their growth. Partnering with bigger names in the industry can provide validation and expand your customer base.
4. **Stay Adaptable**: Supporting industries evolve as the main industry matures. Be prepared to refine your offerings as the industry's needs change. Adaptability ensures that you stay relevant and can continue to support the market even as new competitors emerge.

Exercise: Supporting Strategy Plan

- Write down a potential supporting industry idea you're interested in.
- For each of the tips above, write down an action step you could take to put it into practice. This could include research methods, potential partnership strategies, or ideas for keeping your offerings adaptable.

Final Thoughts on the Power of Supporting Industries

Supporting industries may not always receive the headlines, but they're an essential part of every Gold Rush. By meeting critical needs, they enable pioneers to succeed while building a solid business in the process. Whether you're supplying infrastructure, tools, or technology, being the one who "sells shovels" can yield impressive returns with lower risks.

In an emerging market, sometimes the best path to success isn't leading the charge but supporting those who do. By recognizing gaps in demand, providing valuable resources, and building relationships with industry leaders, you can make a lasting impact without digging for gold yourself. So, when you see a Gold Rush on the horizon, remember that sometimes the best opportunities are in the support systems that make it all possible.

CHAPTER 9: SCALING AND DIVERSIFYING AS THE MARKET MATURES

So, you've established yourself in a promising market, built a loyal customer base, and maybe even gained a reputation as a leader in your space. But as the market matures, it brings new challenges. Competitors start pouring in, consumer expectations evolve, and what once made you unique becomes the industry standard. If you want to stay on top, it's time to adapt, scale, and diversify.

In this chapter, we'll explore strategies for growth as your market matures. We'll look at how to scale efficiently, introduce new offerings, and maintain your edge even as the landscape shifts. Because in a mature market, it's not just about survival—it's about evolving to stay relevant, innovative, and ahead of the game.

Why Scaling Matters in a Maturing Market

Scaling isn't just about getting bigger; it's about expanding your capacity to serve more customers while maintaining quality and efficiency. In a mature market, scaling allows you to capitalize on your established presence, build brand loyalty, and reinforce your market position. But scaling without a strategy can lead to issues, from operational bottlenecks to declining customer satisfaction.

Consider Starbucks' early years. When they first started scaling in the 1990s, they focused on creating a consistent experience across every location. As the market for specialty coffee matured, Starbucks didn't just expand their locations; they scaled with purpose, adding drive-thrus, mobile ordering, and eventually loyalty programs to meet evolving customer expectations. This strategic approach to scaling has kept Starbucks relevant despite an influx of competitors.

Lesson Learned: Scaling is most effective when it's strategic and aligned with customer needs. As your market matures, find ways to grow that enhance your customer experience rather than diluting it.

Step 1: Identifying Opportunities for Scale

Scaling in a mature market is about identifying the aspects of your business that resonate most with customers and amplifying those elements. Here are some areas to consider:

1. **Geographic Expansion**: If your business model is successful in one region, it might be time to expand geographically. Assess where demand for your product or service is growing, and consider setting up operations in those areas.
2. **Improving Operational Efficiency**: As you scale, maintaining efficiency becomes critical. Look for opportunities to streamline your supply chain, enhance inventory management, or automate repetitive tasks. This allows you to handle increased demand without sacrificing quality.
3. **Leveraging Technology for Customer Engagement**: Technology can help you reach and engage customers more effectively. Apps, loyalty programs, and data analytics enable you to provide a personalized experience on a larger scale, keeping customers engaged as the

market grows.

Exercise: Scaling Analysis

- List the top three areas where you think your business could benefit from scaling. Next to each, write down a specific action you could take to expand in that area, such as researching new geographic markets, implementing an inventory management tool, or developing a customer loyalty program.

Case Study: Amazon Web Services—Scaling Through Diversification

When Amazon first launched, it was an online bookstore. But as the e-commerce market matured, Amazon saw an opportunity to leverage its infrastructure in a new way. They introduced Amazon Web Services (AWS), a cloud computing platform that used Amazon's in-house technology to offer storage, hosting, and computing power to other companies. AWS allowed Amazon to scale its brand in a new direction, diversify its offerings, and create a massive new revenue stream.

Today, AWS is a leader in the cloud computing industry, generating billions in revenue and supporting thousands of businesses worldwide. Amazon's strategy to scale through diversification helped them adapt to a maturing e-commerce market by introducing a complementary service.

Lesson Learned: Diversifying doesn't mean abandoning your original business model—it's about leveraging your strengths to enter new markets. By using their existing resources, Amazon expanded in a way that aligned with their capabilities, creating a second major revenue stream.

The Importance of Diversifying in a Mature Market

When markets mature, products and services that were once unique become commonplace, and price competition often intensifies. Diversification allows you to avoid putting all your eggs in one basket and helps you remain adaptable. By introducing complementary products, services, or even entirely new offerings, you're better equipped to meet evolving customer needs and stay competitive.

There are several ways to approach diversification:

1. **Product Line Expansion**: Introduce new products that complement your existing offerings. Apple, for example, started with computers, then moved into portable music players, smartphones, tablets, and even subscription services—all of which complement their original mission.
2. **Vertical Integration**: Take control of more stages in your supply chain, either upstream (e.g., raw materials) or downstream (e.g., distribution). Vertical integration can help reduce costs, improve quality control, and create a more seamless customer experience.
3. **New Market Segments**: Explore new customer segments that you haven't previously targeted. Tesla, for example, started by appealing to high-income consumers with luxury electric vehicles but has since diversified its product range to include more affordable models.

Exercise: Diversification Brainstorm

- Write down three potential ways you could diversify your offerings. For each, consider whether it aligns with your existing strengths, adds value for your customers, and has potential demand in the market.

Case Study: Netflix—From DVD Rentals to Streaming Giant

Netflix began as a DVD rental service by mail, disrupting the video rental market with convenience and competitive pricing. But as digital streaming technology emerged, Netflix saw an opportunity to pivot and adapt. They began offering streaming services, eliminating the need for physical DVDs altogether.

As the market for streaming matured, Netflix diversified again by producing original content, giving them control over a key component of their supply chain. This strategy allowed Netflix to reduce its reliance on third-party content, control quality, and build a loyal audience around exclusive shows and movies.

Lesson Learned: Netflix's shift to streaming and original content illustrates the power of diversification. By anticipating market changes and evolving alongside consumer needs, Netflix not only survived but thrived in a maturing market.

Strategies for Scaling and Diversifying Successfully

Scaling and diversifying sound great on paper, but they require careful planning and execution. Here are strategies for navigating both without losing sight of your brand or overwhelming your resources.

1. **Focus on Core Competencies**: When scaling, don't stray too far from what you're already good at. Leverage your strengths to create additional value, like Amazon did with AWS or Netflix did with original content. This ensures your new offerings are aligned with your brand.
2. **Prioritize Customer Feedback**: As the market matures, customer needs change. Conduct surveys, monitor reviews, and engage with customers to understand what they're looking for. Use this feedback to refine your offerings, introduce new features, and make your products indispensable.
3. **Start Small and Iterate**: When diversifying, start with a pilot or a limited release. This allows you to test demand, gather feedback, and refine your offering before

scaling it. Small, controlled growth reduces the risks associated with diversification and makes it easier to adjust based on real-world results.
4. **Stay Ahead of Competitors**: Keep an eye on what new entrants and established players are doing. If competitors are introducing similar products, find ways to differentiate yourself. Whether through branding, pricing, or added features, set yourself apart by continually innovating.
5. **Develop Scalable Processes**: Scaling can strain your operations. Build processes that can handle increased demand without sacrificing quality. This might mean investing in automation, creating streamlined workflows, or hiring additional staff to ensure you maintain your standards as you grow.

Exercise: Scaling & Diversification Planning

- Choose one area where you could scale and one potential area for diversification. For each, outline specific steps you would take to implement these changes. Consider the resources you'll need, how you'll measure success, and potential adjustments based on customer feedback.

Case Study: Google—Diversifying Through Innovation

Google began as a search engine but quickly diversified into a suite of products and services, from Gmail and Google Maps to Android and YouTube. Google didn't just scale—they continually identified new ways to provide value, allowing them to dominate multiple markets simultaneously. Today, Google is synonymous with search, but they also lead in mobile software, cloud services, and online advertising.

Google's strategy was based on diversifying in ways that complemented their core strength in organizing information and enhancing connectivity. By adding products that kept users within their ecosystem, Google created a seamless experience that met the evolving needs of its users.

Lesson Learned: Google's approach shows that diversification works best when new offerings support and enhance the core business. By staying aligned with its mission, Google scaled and diversified without losing sight of its strengths.

Embracing Agility in a Maturing Market

One of the most important skills in a mature market is agility. Markets don't just grow—they evolve, often in unpredictable ways. Staying agile means being ready to pivot, experiment, and adapt based on what's working and what's not.

An agile approach isn't just reactive; it's proactive. It's about anticipating market changes, trying new ideas, and continuously improving. The companies that thrive in mature markets aren't those that stick rigidly to a single strategy—they're the ones that evolve, embrace feedback, and adapt quickly.

Tips for Staying Agile:

- **Experiment Regularly**: Try out new ideas on a small scale before committing significant resources. Track results and build on what works.
- **Encourage Cross-Department Collaboration**: Sometimes, the best ideas come from outside your core team. Bring together employees from different departments to brainstorm solutions, test new approaches, and share insights.
- **Set Clear Metrics for Success**: Measure your progress with clear metrics. Whether it's customer acquisition, retention, or revenue, use data to guide your decisions and adjust your strategy based on results.

Final Thoughts on Scaling and Diversifying in a Mature Market

Scaling and diversifying are about more than growth—they're

about positioning yourself as a lasting player in an evolving industry. As markets mature, the companies that survive and thrive are those willing to adapt, innovate, and introduce new offerings that resonate with customers. By balancing expansion with quality, staying agile, and embracing the opportunities of diversification, you can evolve alongside your market and maintain a competitive edge.

In the end, the goal isn't just to grow bigger; it's to grow smarter. By scaling thoughtfully and diversifying with purpose, you ensure that your business remains relevant and resilient—capable of meeting changing needs, overcoming new challenges, and continuing to thrive as the market reaches its next phase.

Part IV: Long-Term Strategies for Sustaining Wealth

CHAPTER 10: INNOVATE OR GET LEFT BEHIND

If there's one rule that applies to every business in every industry, it's this: innovate or get left behind. In fast-paced markets, the only way to stay relevant is by continually evolving, experimenting, and pushing boundaries. Even the most successful companies can't afford to rest on their laurels. Why? Because as soon as you stop innovating, you're inviting competitors to swoop in, offering something fresher, faster, or simply better.

In this chapter, we'll dive into the necessity of ongoing innovation and explore examples of companies that adapted to changing landscapes as well as those that failed to keep pace. You'll learn strategies for building a culture of innovation, fostering creativity, and ensuring that your business remains competitive—even as the market shifts beneath your feet.

Why Innovation Matters in Fast-Paced Markets

Innovation isn't just a buzzword; it's a survival strategy. In today's business world, technology and consumer preferences change rapidly. What worked last year might feel outdated today, and your competitors are always looking for ways to offer something better. When a company stops evolving, they become vulnerable to competitors who aren't afraid to push boundaries.

Think about the tech industry. With advancements happening almost daily, even tech giants like Apple, Google, and Microsoft know they must constantly innovate to stay on top. They don't just release new products—they improve and reinvent existing ones to stay relevant. And it's this commitment to ongoing innovation that helps them maintain market dominance.

Lesson Learned: In a fast-paced market, innovation isn't optional. It's a necessary strategy to stay relevant, competitive, and resilient as the market evolves.

Case Study: Netflix—From DVD Rentals to Streaming Pioneer

Netflix's story is often cited as a prime example of successful innovation. Originally a DVD rental-by-mail service, Netflix disrupted the traditional video rental market by offering a more convenient way to rent movies. But as the industry changed and streaming technology emerged, Netflix took another bold step and transitioned to a streaming platform.

However, their innovation didn't stop there. As streaming became the norm, Netflix began producing original content, from "House of Cards" to "Stranger Things," positioning itself as both a distributor and creator. This constant evolution allowed Netflix to stay relevant, attract new customers, and fend off competition from other streaming services. Today, they continue to lead the streaming industry, having successfully adapted through multiple market shifts.

Lesson Learned: Netflix's willingness to reinvent itself allowed them to stay at the forefront of the entertainment industry. Their story shows that innovation isn't a one-time change—it's a continuous process of adapting, evolving, and staying ahead.

Recognizing When It's Time to Innovate

Knowing *when* to innovate is just as important as knowing *how* to do it. Successful companies are often those that can sense when their products, services, or strategies are starting to lose relevance and are quick to pivot or enhance them. Here are some signs that it may be time to innovate:

1. **Customer Demand Shifts**: If you notice customers starting to demand features or services you don't offer, it's a sign that expectations are changing and it's time to adapt.
2. **Increasing Competition**: If competitors are starting to outperform you with better products, pricing, or user experience, it's time to rethink your approach to avoid losing market share.
3. **Industry Advancements**: Major technological or regulatory changes in your industry often open doors to new opportunities. Staying updated on these shifts can reveal areas ripe for innovation.
4. **Growth Plateau**: If your growth is stagnating, it may be because your products or services no longer feel fresh or valuable. Innovation can help you capture renewed interest and re-energize your brand.

Exercise: Innovation Radar

- Identify three areas in your business or product that could benefit from innovation. Think about customer demand, competitors, and any advancements in your industry.
- Write down potential innovations or improvements for each area, and prioritize the one that could have the most impact on your business.

Case Study: Kodak—The Failure to Evolve

Kodak was once a giant in the photography industry, but they failed to innovate when digital photography emerged. Ironically, Kodak actually invented the first digital camera in 1975 but chose not to pursue it, fearing it would cannibalize their profitable film business. Instead of leading the digital photography revolution, Kodak resisted it, allowing competitors like Sony and Canon to dominate the market.

As digital photography became mainstream, Kodak's film business plummeted, and their lack of adaptation led to a steady decline. Eventually, Kodak filed for bankruptcy in 2012—a cautionary tale of what happens when a company refuses to innovate.

Lesson Learned: Kodak's story is a stark reminder that clinging to outdated business models can be disastrous. Innovation might seem risky, but failing to innovate is often riskier. Companies that prioritize short-term gains over long-term relevance are likely to get left behind.

Building a Culture of Innovation

To stay relevant in a fast-paced market, innovation must be woven into the fabric of your company culture. A culture of innovation encourages employees to think creatively, take calculated risks, and continuously improve. Here are some ways to foster innovation within your organization:

1. **Encourage Experimentation**: Create an environment where employees feel safe to try new ideas, even if they don't always succeed. Some of the best innovations come from trial and error, so emphasize learning over perfection.
2. **Reward Creativity**: Recognize and reward employees who bring fresh ideas to the table. This could be through incentives, recognition programs, or simply celebrating wins (big and small) at team meetings.
3. **Involve Diverse Perspectives**: Diverse teams bring a broader range of ideas, experiences, and viewpoints. Foster an inclusive environment where everyone feels comfortable sharing their thoughts, regardless of their

role or background.
4. **Embrace Feedback Loops**: Encourage feedback from both customers and employees. Customer feedback reveals how your product could be improved, while employee feedback offers insights into your processes, helping identify areas for innovation.

Exercise: Innovation Culture Checklist

- Rate your company on each of the points above, from 1 (needs improvement) to 5 (strong culture). Identify one area where you could improve your innovation culture.
- Brainstorm ways to implement improvements, such as starting a monthly "innovation session" where team members can pitch ideas.

Case Study: Apple—A Culture of Innovation

Apple is one of the world's most innovative companies, not just because of its products but because of its approach to creativity. Under Steve Jobs, Apple fostered a culture that encouraged ambitious ideas, intense collaboration, and a relentless focus on design and user experience. Apple employees were encouraged to think differently and push the boundaries of what technology could do.

This culture of innovation led to the creation of iconic products like the iPod, iPhone, and iPad, transforming entire industries. Even today, Apple continues to innovate with new products and services, from Apple Watch to Apple Music, showing that their commitment to creativity has lasting power.

Lesson Learned: Apple's success isn't just about groundbreaking products; it's about a culture that values innovation at every level. By encouraging creativity and valuing bold ideas, they created a lasting legacy of innovation.

Staying Agile in a Changing Market

In fast-paced markets, agility is key. Companies that can quickly respond to new trends, technologies, and consumer needs have a better chance of staying competitive. Being agile doesn't mean you're constantly making drastic changes—it means you're open to adjusting your approach based on feedback, data, and market shifts. Here's how to stay agile in a changing market:

1. **Set Short-Term Goals**: While long-term vision is essential, short-term goals allow you to be flexible and adapt quickly. Reevaluate goals regularly to ensure they align with current market conditions.
2. **Monitor Industry Trends**: Keep a close eye on your industry's trends, even if they don't seem directly relevant at first. Sometimes, an unrelated trend can inspire new ideas or reveal opportunities for innovation.
3. **Implement Rapid Prototyping**: Instead of spending months perfecting an idea, focus on developing a prototype or MVP (Minimum Viable Product) quickly. This allows you to test ideas in real-time and adjust based on actual user feedback.
4. **Empower Decision-Making**: Allow your team to make decisions and act on opportunities quickly. The faster you can respond to new insights, the more agile your company will be.

Exercise: Agility Assessment

- Review your current business processes. Identify one area where agility could be improved (e.g., decision-making speed, prototyping new products, or responding to customer feedback).
- Write down one action step you could take to enhance agility in that area, such as implementing weekly progress check-ins or streamlining your approval process for new initiatives.

Case Study: Blockbuster—The Cost of Inflexibility

Blockbuster once dominated the video rental industry, but their inflexibility and refusal to adapt led to their downfall. When Netflix introduced a subscription-based DVD rental model by mail, Blockbuster dismissed it as a niche offering. Later, Netflix launched a streaming service, further capitalizing on the shift to digital content. Despite several chances to evolve, Blockbuster clung to its outdated model of brick-and-mortar rentals.

Eventually, Netflix's innovative model, combined with Blockbuster's reluctance to change, led to the latter's bankruptcy. Blockbuster's story illustrates the dangers of inflexibility in a changing market. Their inability to adapt allowed Netflix to lead the streaming revolution and become a media giant.

Lesson Learned: In a fast-paced market, flexibility is essential. Businesses that resist change or ignore emerging trends risk being left behind. Adapting quickly to market shifts can make the difference between thriving and becoming obsolete.

Fostering Continuous Innovation

Innovation shouldn't be a one-time initiative; it needs to be a continuous effort. Companies that innovate regularly are more resilient, adaptable, and better equipped to meet customer needs. Here are ways to keep innovation alive in your organization:

1. **Schedule Regular Brainstorming Sessions**: Make innovation part of your team's routine. Hold regular brainstorming sessions to generate ideas, address challenges, and explore new approaches.
2. **Allocate Resources for R&D**: Set aside a budget for research and development. Even small investments in R&D can yield significant innovations, whether it's process improvements, new products, or enhanced services.
3. **Celebrate Innovation Wins**: Recognize and celebrate

innovative ideas that have positively impacted the company. This reinforces the value of creativity and motivates employees to keep thinking outside the box.
4. **Invest in Professional Development**: Encourage employees to attend conferences, take courses, and stay updated on industry trends. Exposure to new ideas and skills can fuel innovative thinking and help the company stay competitive.

Exercise: Innovation Continuity Plan

- Choose one strategy from the list above that resonates most with your organization.
- Outline a specific action plan to implement this strategy, such as scheduling quarterly brainstorming sessions or setting up a budget for R&D. This will help you foster an environment of continuous innovation.

Final Thoughts on Innovating to Stay Ahead

In a world that's constantly evolving, staying relevant means never settling. Innovation isn't just a nice-to-have—it's a must-have for businesses that want to thrive in fast-paced markets. By building a culture of creativity, staying agile, and continuously investing in innovation, you can ensure that your business remains competitive, resilient, and ready for whatever comes next.

The companies that survive and thrive are those willing to adapt, embrace change, and push the boundaries of what's possible. So, as you navigate your journey in a fast-paced market, remember: the future belongs to the innovators. And with the right mindset, resources, and commitment, there's no reason that can't be you.

CHAPTER 11: INVESTING IN FUTURE-BASED MARKETS

Imagine if you'd had the foresight to invest in the internet in the early '90s, or e-commerce before Amazon became a household name. Today, future-based markets like artificial intelligence, space exploration, and biotech offer similar opportunities. These fields aren't just trends—they're likely to reshape the world as we know it. And by positioning yourself strategically, you can play a role in building that future while capitalizing on transformative changes.

In this chapter, we'll explore strategies for investing in these future-based markets and provide exercises to help you spot early indicators of shifts in industries and consumer behaviors. Because in a world that's constantly evolving, knowing how to recognize the next big thing is invaluable.

Why Future-Based Markets Matter

Future-based markets are those with the potential to change industries, economies, and lives. They're driven by advancements in technology, science, and innovation, and they cater to needs that will only become more relevant as the world progresses. Investing in these markets doesn't just offer potential financial rewards—it positions you at the forefront of tomorrow's economy. By getting in early, you establish yourself as a key player, gaining valuable insights and influencing the market's direction.

Consider artificial intelligence. A decade ago, it was a niche interest. Today, it's transforming industries from healthcare to finance, and it's predicted to be one of the biggest economic drivers of the 21st century. Investing early in AI means being part of a movement that will shape the future of work, communication, and even decision-making.

Lesson Learned: Future-based markets allow you to capitalize on trends that will become essential over time. While they carry risks, they also offer unparalleled opportunities for growth, influence, and impact.

Key Future-Based Markets to Watch

Here are a few future-based markets with significant potential. These industries are still developing, which makes them both exciting and unpredictable, but early movers have the chance to shape their future and reap the rewards.

1. **Artificial Intelligence (AI)**: AI has applications across nearly every industry, from healthcare diagnostics and customer service to robotics and autonomous vehicles. The market is projected to grow exponentially, with AI integration becoming essential for companies to stay competitive.
2. **Space Exploration and Commercialization**: SpaceX, Blue Origin, and NASA are all working to make space exploration accessible and economically viable. The space economy isn't just about launching rockets; it includes satellite technology, space tourism, asteroid mining, and even colonizing other planets.
3. **Biotechnology and Genetic Engineering**: Biotech is transforming medicine and agriculture, with breakthroughs in gene therapy, CRISPR, and synthetic biology offering solutions for previously untreatable

diseases. It has vast potential in healthcare, food production, and environmental preservation.
4. **Clean Energy and Sustainability**: As climate change continues to be a pressing concern, clean energy sources like solar, wind, and hydrogen, along with sustainable technologies, are becoming crucial. This market offers both immediate relevance and long-term growth potential.
5. **Quantum Computing**: Though still in its early stages, quantum computing promises to revolutionize problem-solving, optimization, and data processing, with applications in cryptography, pharmaceuticals, and complex simulations.

Exercise: Future Market Research

- Choose one of the markets above that interests you most. Spend 15 minutes researching recent developments in that industry and write down three key takeaways, trends, or predictions.
- Based on your research, brainstorm one potential business or investment opportunity related to that market. This could be a tool, service, or partnership that aligns with future demand.

Case Study: Tesla—Leading the Future of Clean Energy and Mobility

Tesla is one of the most successful examples of investing in a future-based market. When Elon Musk took over the company in 2004, electric vehicles (EVs) were considered impractical and niche. But Musk believed in a future where clean energy and sustainable transportation would be essential. Tesla's commitment to innovation allowed them to bring EVs into the mainstream, and today, they're leading the industry with advancements in battery technology, self-driving features, and energy storage.

Tesla didn't just invest in a product; they invested in a vision. By positioning themselves as leaders in the clean energy and mobility sectors, they influenced regulatory policies, shaped consumer expectations, and set standards for an entire industry.

Lesson Learned: Investing in future-based markets means taking a leap of faith, but it also means influencing the industry as it grows. Tesla's success highlights the power of aligning with emerging trends and building a brand around forward-thinking ideals.

Spotting Early Signs of Shifts in Industries

One of the keys to investing in future-based markets is learning to recognize early indicators of change. By spotting these shifts, you can position yourself strategically before others catch on. Here are a few ways to stay ahead:

1. **Follow Thought Leaders and Innovators**: Industry pioneers and thought leaders are often the first to recognize emerging trends. Follow people like Elon Musk, Ray Kurzweil, or Tim Urban, and subscribe to publications that cover cutting-edge technology and science.
2. **Track Research and Patents**: Research institutions and companies filing patents for new technology often indicate what's next. Resources like Google Patents, research journals, and industry reports can provide insight into what technologies are in the pipeline.
3. **Monitor Regulatory Changes**: Governments and regulatory bodies often shape market trends through policy. For instance, clean energy regulations and subsidies have accelerated the adoption of solar and wind technologies. Staying aware of these changes can give you a sense of where industries are headed.
4. **Watch for Changes in Consumer Behavior**: When consumers start adopting new behaviors, it often signals a shift. For example, the rise of mobile devices and social media created a demand for mobile-first applications

and services. Monitoring shifts in consumer behavior can help you understand emerging needs and preferences.

Exercise: Shift Analysis

- Choose an industry you're interested in and note any recent changes you've seen, whether in consumer behavior, technological advances, or regulatory policies.
- Write down one or two ways these changes could impact the industry in the next five years. Based on your observations, consider any opportunities or threats these shifts might create for your business or investment strategy.

Case Study: IBM—Pivoting to Quantum Computing

IBM is one of the oldest tech companies in the world, yet they've remained relevant by continuously adapting to new technologies. Over the past few years, IBM has invested heavily in quantum computing, a field that promises to revolutionize computing as we know it. IBM Quantum, a division within IBM, is working to make quantum computing accessible to businesses and researchers.

By investing in quantum technology early, IBM positioned itself as a leader in a future-based market, developing expertise and influence that will benefit them as the technology matures. IBM's proactive approach highlights the importance of diversifying within future-based markets to ensure long-term relevance.

Lesson Learned: IBM's focus on quantum computing shows that companies don't have to rely on existing products or markets to remain competitive. By investing in a promising but nascent field, IBM is preparing to lead in an entirely new sector.

Strategies for Positioning Yourself in Future-Based Markets

Once you've identified a promising market, it's time to develop a strategy for establishing yourself within it. Positioning in a future-based market requires a blend of research, adaptability, and forward-thinking. Here's how to make the most of your investment:

1. **Build Specialized Knowledge**: Future-based markets are complex and require in-depth understanding. Investing in education, research, or hiring experts can give you an edge and help you make informed decisions.
2. **Collaborate with Innovators**: Partnerships with other companies, startups, or research institutions can provide access to new technologies, funding, and resources. Collaboration can speed up your growth and open doors to new opportunities.
3. **Stay Agile**: Future-based markets evolve quickly, so agility is essential. Be willing to pivot, experiment, and adapt based on new developments. Flexibility will allow you to navigate the uncertainties of an emerging industry.
4. **Focus on Long-Term Value**: While it's tempting to chase short-term gains, future-based markets are more likely to yield long-term rewards. Stay committed to your vision, and make decisions that will add value over time.

Exercise: Positioning Plan

- Choose a future-based market you're interested in. Write down two to three steps you could take to position yourself within that market, such as building specialized knowledge, identifying potential partners, or developing a flexible business model.
- Set a timeline for each step to help you stay focused and proactive as you enter this new space.

Case Study: CRISPR Therapeutics—Betting on Genetic Engineering

CRISPR Therapeutics is a biotech company focused on gene-editing technology. CRISPR (short for Clustered Regularly Interspaced Short Palindromic Repeats) is a groundbreaking technology that allows scientists to edit genes with unprecedented precision. By investing in this field, CRISPR Therapeutics positioned itself at the forefront of genetic engineering, with potential applications in treating genetic disorders, agriculture, and even environmental sustainability.

Though gene-editing is still in its early stages, CRISPR Therapeutics has made significant strides by focusing on collaboration, research, and partnerships with academic institutions and biotech companies. Their proactive approach and commitment to long-term impact have solidified their position as a leader in a future-based market.

Lesson Learned: CRISPR Therapeutics' success underscores the importance of staying focused and investing in foundational research in future-based markets. By betting on a transformative technology, they're positioned to benefit from advancements in gene-editing that could have profound societal impact.

Exercises for Spotting Future-Based Market Shifts

Here are some exercises to help you build your "future vision" muscles and recognize emerging opportunities.

1. **Trend Spotting**: Every day for a week, read one article related to technology, science, or market trends. Write down any trends or innovations that stand out, and ask yourself if they indicate a potential market shift.
2. **Consumer Needs Analysis**: Think of three current consumer needs or frustrations and consider how they might evolve. What future-based markets could potentially meet these needs? Brainstorm one product, service, or technology that could address each need.

3. **Competitor Watch**: Pick a company that interests you and track any new initiatives, products, or partnerships they announce over the next month. This can give you insight into where they see the future of their industry heading—and potential opportunities for your own positioning.

Final Thoughts on Investing in Future-Based Markets

Investing in future-based markets isn't without risks, but it offers the chance to be part of something transformative. By staying informed, adaptable, and proactive, you can position yourself to lead in industries that will shape the future. Whether you're interested in AI, space exploration, biotech, or something else entirely, remember that the key is to balance strategic positioning with a commitment to learning, growth, and innovation.

In the end, success in future-based markets comes down to one thing: vision. And if you're willing to invest in that vision, you'll not only play a role in building tomorrow—you'll be ready to profit from it, too.

CHAPTER 12: BUILDING RESILIENT WEALTH

Congratulations—you've made it this far. You've leveraged new opportunities, positioned yourself in emerging markets, and started seeing real gains. But wealth isn't just about making money; it's about keeping it, growing it, and passing it on. Building resilient wealth means creating a foundation that will last beyond today's trends and can support you and future generations in the long term.

In this chapter, we'll dive into strategies for transforming your initial success into long-term wealth. From smart investments and strategic acquisitions to sustainable wealth-building practices, this chapter will guide you in transitioning from active wealth-building to strategies for resilience and generational prosperity.

Why Building Resilient Wealth Matters

Creating wealth is one thing, but making it last is a different story. Short-term wealth can come from a big business win, investment, or inheritance, but without a plan, it's easy to lose it as fast as it was gained. Building resilient wealth isn't about making money quickly; it's about protecting and growing what you have so that it provides security and opportunities well into the future.

Consider the family fortunes that have endured for generations. Families like the Rockefellers, Vanderbilts, and Rothschilds didn't just amass wealth—they established practices, trusts, and diversified portfolios to preserve it across generations. They used smart investments, strategic partnerships, and conservative spending to ensure that their wealth would benefit not just them but their descendants.

Lesson Learned: Building resilient wealth is about the long game. It requires patience, strategy, and the ability to think beyond immediate gains. With a plan in place, you can transform your initial successes into a foundation for lasting prosperity.

Transforming Gains into Long-Term Wealth

The first step in building resilient wealth is to transform short-term gains into long-term assets. This involves smart allocation, diversification, and making strategic choices that increase value over time. Here's how to do it:

1. **Reinvest in High-Value Assets**: After an initial success, resist the urge to spend. Instead, focus on reinvesting your gains in assets that appreciate over time. Real estate, stocks, bonds, and high-quality businesses are examples of assets that can increase wealth over the long term.
2. **Diversify Your Portfolio**: Don't put all your eggs in one basket. Diversifying across different asset classes reduces risk and allows you to benefit from different types of market growth. This might include a mix of stocks, bonds, real estate, and possibly alternative investments like art or cryptocurrency.
3. **Focus on Stable, Cash-Generating Investments**: Assets that generate passive income—like rental properties, dividend stocks, or income-generating businesses—can provide a steady stream of income that supports

wealth preservation. By reinvesting this passive income, you can continue to grow wealth sustainably.

Exercise: Wealth Transformation Plan

- Write down your current assets and evaluate which ones have the potential for long-term growth. Identify at least two assets you could add to diversify your portfolio.
- Create a plan for reinvesting a portion of your gains in cash-generating or growth-oriented assets. Set a timeline and specific goals for building a balanced portfolio.

Case Study: Warren Buffett—Master of Resilient Wealth-Building

Warren Buffett is often regarded as one of the greatest investors of all time. What's his secret? Buffett's wealth-building strategy is simple but effective: focus on long-term value. Instead of seeking quick profits, he invests in companies with strong fundamentals, reliable cash flows, and lasting growth potential. His patience, discipline, and value-oriented approach have enabled him to build one of the world's largest personal fortunes.

Buffett's strategy is a masterclass in resilient wealth-building. He doesn't chase trends or overextend himself with risky investments. Instead, he looks for undervalued companies, invests in them for the long haul, and lets the power of compound growth do the work.

Lesson Learned: Wealth that lasts is wealth that's built patiently. Following Buffett's example, focus on stable, long-term investments, reinvest your earnings, and allow compounding to build wealth gradually.

Building Wealth Through Strategic Acquisitions and Partnerships

In addition to traditional investments, strategic acquisitions and partnerships can play a significant role in resilient wealth-building. By acquiring companies or forming partnerships that align with your strengths, you can expand your influence, generate new income streams, and reduce risk.

1. **Acquisitions for Expansion**: Acquiring smaller businesses that complement your current holdings can help you expand your reach, tap into new markets, or streamline operations. Look for businesses that offer synergies, such as overlapping customer bases or complementary services.
2. **Partnerships for Diversification**: Strategic partnerships allow you to diversify without a full commitment. For example, you might partner with a company in a different industry to share resources, combine expertise, or co-develop a new product. Partnerships create mutually beneficial opportunities that strengthen both parties.
3. **Leveraging Private Equity or Venture Capital**: As your wealth grows, you might consider investing in private equity or venture capital. These investments are often higher-risk, but they offer potential for high returns and access to emerging markets or innovative companies. By investing in promising startups, you diversify your portfolio and have the chance to support companies that could shape the future.

Exercise: Strategic Acquisition & Partnership Plan

- Think of one or two companies or types of businesses that could complement your current investments. Consider areas where you might want to expand, diversify, or enhance your influence.
- Outline potential benefits of acquiring or partnering with these companies. Identify synergies, new markets, or cost savings they could bring.

Case Study: Google's Strategic Acquisitions

Google's acquisition strategy is a powerful example of using acquisitions to build resilient wealth. Since its founding, Google has acquired hundreds of companies, including YouTube, Android, and DoubleClick. Each acquisition allowed Google to diversify its offerings, enter new markets, and reduce reliance on a single revenue stream (e.g., search advertising).

By acquiring companies with long-term value, Google strengthened its ecosystem and built a diverse portfolio of products and services. This diversification allowed Google to grow steadily while shielding itself from market volatility in any one area.

Lesson Learned: Strategic acquisitions allow you to grow your influence, diversify, and establish a lasting presence in multiple markets. When done thoughtfully, acquisitions can significantly enhance resilient wealth-building.

Transitioning from Active to Sustainable Wealth-Building

As your wealth grows, it's essential to shift from active wealth-building to strategies that focus on sustainability. Sustainable wealth-building includes strategies that ensure your assets retain value and provide consistent returns without requiring constant management.

1. **Set Up Trusts and Estates**: Trusts can protect your assets, reduce taxes, and ensure that your wealth is distributed according to your wishes. Estate planning is crucial for preserving wealth across generations and minimizing legal complexities for heirs.
2. **Implement Risk Management**: Protecting your wealth requires managing risks. Consider insurance policies for valuable assets, emergency funds, and portfolio hedging strategies to guard against market down-

turns.

3. **Establish a Wealth Preservation Strategy**: Wealth preservation involves balancing growth with protection. This can mean shifting part of your portfolio to low-risk investments, such as bonds or stable real estate, while maintaining some exposure to higher-growth assets.

Exercise: Sustainable Wealth Checklist

- List the steps you need to take to transition from active wealth-building to sustainable wealth strategies. This might include setting up a trust, developing a more conservative investment approach, or meeting with a financial advisor.
- Set goals for each area and create a timeline for implementing your sustainable wealth-building plan.

Case Study: The Rockefeller Legacy—Generational Wealth Preservation

The Rockefeller family, one of America's wealthiest dynasties, built their fortune in the oil industry. But their wealth didn't just come from amassing money; it was preserved and passed down through smart investments, trusts, and foundations. The Rockefeller family's wealth-building model includes diversified investments, estate planning, and philanthropy, all designed to create sustainable wealth for future generations.

By setting up trusts and emphasizing long-term preservation, the Rockefellers established a financial legacy that continues to thrive. Their strategy focused not only on growth but on preserving wealth in a way that would last for generations.

Lesson Learned: Building resilient wealth requires not just growth but protection and sustainability. By establishing trusts, diversifying, and planning for the future, the Rockefellers created a model of generational wealth that endures.

Developing Generational Wealth Strategies

Generational wealth isn't just about leaving money behind; it's about creating a legacy. To build generational wealth, focus on strategies that will support, educate, and empower future generations.

1. **Financial Education for Heirs**: Teach your family members about financial literacy, investing, and wealth management. Providing heirs with the knowledge and skills they need to manage wealth responsibly can help prevent common pitfalls.
2. **Philanthropy and Giving Back**: Philanthropy allows you to leave a positive impact on society while instilling values of generosity and purpose. Charitable foundations, donor-advised funds, and scholarship programs are ways to create a lasting legacy.
3. **Create a Family Mission Statement**: A family mission statement defines your values, goals, and approach to wealth. It provides a guiding framework for future generations, helping them stay aligned with your vision while managing wealth responsibly.

Exercise: Generational Wealth Blueprint

- Create a generational wealth plan that includes financial education, philanthropic goals, and a family mission statement. Write down specific ways to educate your heirs, such as setting up a trust, organizing family meetings, or developing a family giving plan.
- Outline steps to implement your generational wealth strategy, such as identifying key philanthropic causes or establishing a timeline for introducing heirs to financial management principles.

Final Thoughts on Building Resilient Wealth

Building resilient wealth isn't a quick process—it's a journey that requires patience, discipline, and a commitment to long-term growth. By reinvesting in high-value assets, establishing strategic partnerships, and planning for future generations, you can transform initial gains into a legacy that endures. Remember, true wealth is about more than just money—it's about creating opportunities, security, and impact that can benefit you, your family, and society.

So, as you continue building wealth, think beyond the immediate gains. Focus on the steps you can take today to establish a legacy of resilience, purpose, and prosperity for years to come.

CONCLUSION: KEY TAKEAWAYS FROM THE GOLD RUSH

As we reach the end of this journey, let's take a step back and reflect on the incredible opportunities history has shown us—lessons that continue to be relevant today. The Gold Rush may be long over, but its wisdom endures. The same principles that guided those early pioneers toward wealth are alive in today's digital age, clean energy revolution, biotech innovations, and beyond.

From spotting the first glimmers of a Gold Rush to creating resilient wealth, this book has explored the full scope of wealth creation. At its core, there are six "absolute truths" that ring as true today as they did in the days of pickaxes and gold pans. Understanding these truths—and committing to their pursuit—will put you on the path to a legacy of wealth, resilience, and purpose.

The Six Absolute Truths of Wealth Creation

Here's a final look at the timeless principles that can help you build wealth and create lasting impact, regardless of how the market changes:

1. **They'll Doubt You First**: Pioneers are rarely greeted with applause. The world may doubt your vision and question your sanity, but that's the price of leading rather than following. Believe in your purpose, and let

skepticism fuel your determination.
2. **Pioneers Prove the Concept**: Those who enter a market first take on the challenge of proving what's possible. By being first, you test the waters, set the standards, and create the roadmap others will follow. Embrace the thrill of exploring uncharted territory—it's where the greatest opportunities lie.
3. **New Money Levels the Playing Field**: Every Gold Rush levels the playing field. In a new market, anyone can enter, regardless of status, background, or resources. This is the chance to build a business or brand that stands on its own merit, not on pre-existing power.
4. **The First Technology Becomes the Old Technology**: The first way is rarely the only way. As markets mature, competitors, new technology, and innovation always emerge. Stay agile, anticipate change, and be willing to adapt—because evolution is essential for survival.
5. **Supporting Industries Create the Bulk of New Wealth**: The ones who supply the tools, infrastructure, or services for a booming market often achieve the most enduring success. When you support those in pursuit of "gold," you're tapping into a wealth of opportunity without bearing all the risks.
6. **A Permanent Change in the Ecosystem Always Comes Out of It**: Every Gold Rush leaves a lasting impact, reshaping industries, economies, and lives. By understanding the ripple effects of a booming market, you position yourself to adapt, innovate, and remain relevant long after the initial rush fades.

Building Your Own Path to Opportunity

The Gold Rush may be over, but the spirit of discovery and ambition that fueled it is alive and well. The truth is, we live in a world where Gold Rush opportunities are constantly emerging, whether in technology, healthcare, sustainability, or new media. These opportunities may not always be obvious, but they're waiting to be uncovered by those with the vision, resilience, and drive to pursue them.

As you step forward, remember the principles in this book. Approach each new opportunity with curiosity and creativity. Build a network of supporters and mentors. Trust in your instincts. Embrace failure as a part of the journey. And above all, be willing to innovate, adapt, and evolve.

Final Words of Encouragement

Wealth creation isn't just about money—it's about having the freedom to pursue your vision, the power to impact lives, and the ability to shape a legacy. It's about seeing potential where others see obstacles and taking calculated risks where others stay in their comfort zones.

So, whether you're an experienced entrepreneur or just starting, trust in your ability to spot the next big opportunity. Equip yourself with the right tools, surround yourself with the right people, and be prepared to blaze your own trail. Remember, the future belongs to those willing to pursue it. And you, with the principles of wealth creation on your side, are more than ready to claim it.

Go forth, seek out your Gold Rush, and make your mark on the world. The next big opportunity is out there—waiting for someone bold enough to seize it. Why not let that someone be you?

APPENDIX

Resources for Aspiring Entrepreneurs

Exploring a new market or industry can be overwhelming without the right resources. This section includes recommended books, articles, websites, and tools to help you stay informed, inspired, and equipped as you navigate the next big opportunity.

Recommended Books

1. **"The Lean Startup" by Eric Ries**: A go-to guide for launching new ventures, with a focus on creating sustainable business models through validated learning and adaptability.
2. **"Zero to One" by Peter Thiel and Blake Masters**: A look at building revolutionary businesses from scratch, with insights on innovation, market domination, and entrepreneurial vision.
3. **"Blue Ocean Strategy" by W. Chan Kim and Renée Mauborgne**: This classic book provides insights on creating uncontested market space and building a lasting brand without competing directly.
4. **"The Innovator's Dilemma" by Clayton Christensen**: Explores why successful companies can fall behind in fast-changing markets and how new entrants can leverage innovation to their advantage.
5. **"Principles: Life and Work" by Ray Dalio**: Combines life and business advice with valuable insights on risk, decision-making, and achieving long-term goals.

Articles and Websites

- **Harvard Business Review (hbr.org)**: A treasure trove of articles on entrepreneurship, innovation, and strategic thinking.
- **TechCrunch (techcrunch.com)**: Covers technology trends, funding updates, and emerging companies across various sectors.
- **Crunchbase (crunchbase.com)**: Offers data on start-ups, acquisitions, and venture funding, making it an excellent tool for market research.
- **CB Insights (cbinsights.com)**: Provides reports and data-driven articles on technology, business trends, and future-based markets.

Tools for Market Research

- **Google Trends (trends.google.com)**: Allows you to track interest in specific topics and keywords over time, revealing market shifts and emerging trends.
- **Statista (statista.com)**: Offers statistical data across industries, providing insight into market sizes, consumer behavior, and growth projections.
- **PitchBook (pitchbook.com)**: A resource for in-depth data on venture capital, private equity, and M&A activity.
- **Quid (quid.com)**: A data visualization tool that reveals hidden connections in data, useful for mapping industry trends and spotting emerging opportunities.
- **Keyword Planner (ads.google.com)**: Google's tool can help identify popular search terms, aiding in understanding customer interests and potential demand in new markets.

Gold Rush Glossary

Here's a glossary of terms that can help entrepreneurs exploring new markets better understand key concepts:

- **First-Mover Advantage**: The benefits gained by being the first to enter a new market, including brand establishment and reduced competition.
- **Future-Based Market**: An emerging market likely to play a significant role in shaping the future, such as artificial intelligence, clean energy, or biotech.
- **Gold Rush Opportunity**: A period of high demand and growth in a new market where early entrants have significant potential for wealth creation.
- **Market Saturation**: A point at which a market is so well-served that further growth is limited, typically leading to increased competition and reduced profitability.
- **Minimum Viable Product (MVP)**: A basic version of a new product that is created to test a market before full-scale launch, allowing for early feedback and adaptation.
- **Pivot**: A significant shift in business strategy, often in response to market feedback or new insights.
- **Risk Mitigation**: Strategies designed to minimize potential risks in business, such as diversification, hedging, or insurance.
- **Scalability**: The ability of a business to grow and serve a larger customer base without a corresponding increase in operational costs.
- **Supporting Industry**: Industries that provide essential tools, resources, or infrastructure for the primary players in a market (e.g., shovel sellers in the Gold Rush).
- **Venture Capital**: A form of private equity financing provided by investors to startups and small businesses with growth potential in exchange for equity.

Case Studies in Modern Gold Rushes

For entrepreneurs seeking further inspiration, here are some additional examples of successful entrepreneurs who recognized and capitalized on emerging markets:

1. **Elon Musk and Tesla's Entry into Electric Vehicles (EVs)**
   Elon Musk's Tesla has become a defining force in the EV market, with early recognition of the shift toward clean energy. Tesla's focus on building a brand around sustainability and high-performance vehicles positioned it as the dominant player in a rapidly growing market. Tesla's success in the EV market has not only propelled the company's growth but has also influenced global energy policies and consumer behaviors around electric mobility.
2. **Evan Spiegel and Snapchat's Appeal to Gen Z**
   Snapchat entered the social media market with a unique, ephemeral approach to content sharing, which resonated strongly with younger audiences. Evan Spiegel recognized the shift in user behavior toward privacy, quick communication, and creative expression, leveraging these trends to build a platform with a highly engaged, loyal user base. Snapchat's entry has influenced social media trends and even larger platforms like Instagram and Facebook to adopt similar features.
3. **Patagonia and the Rise of Sustainable Fashion**
   Long before sustainability became mainstream, Patagonia positioned itself as an environmentally-conscious brand, prioritizing quality and ethical production practices. Patagonia's strategy allowed them to build a loyal following of environmentally-minded consumers and establish a reputation as a leader in sustainable fashion. Today, as consumers become more focused on sustainability, Patagonia's early positioning and commitment to ethical practices continue to distinguish the brand.
4. **Shopify and the E-Commerce Boom**

As the e-commerce market grew, Shopify emerged as a go-to platform for small and medium-sized businesses to create online stores. Shopify provided the infrastructure, tools, and support that budding entrepreneurs needed to enter the online retail space. Their success demonstrates the power of supporting industries in emerging markets. By providing essential tools for e-commerce, Shopify became an industry leader while avoiding direct competition with individual sellers.

5. **Beyond Meat and the Plant-Based Food Market**
Beyond Meat was among the first companies to bring plant-based meat alternatives to a mainstream audience. As consumer interest in healthier, sustainable diets grew, Beyond Meat capitalized on the opportunity to create a product that mimicked traditional meat but with fewer environmental impacts. Beyond Meat's approach to innovation in the food industry has helped legitimize the plant-based food market and create new demand for alternative proteins.

These case studies showcase modern entrepreneurs who leveraged Gold Rush opportunities to build impactful businesses. Whether they pioneered an industry or provided the essential tools that allowed others to succeed, each of these leaders recognized an emerging need and built a lasting legacy.

With these resources, terms, and case studies, you're equipped with a toolkit to guide your journey in any market—whether you're leading the charge or supporting those who do. Remember, every Gold Rush has room for those with vision, drive, and the courage to take the first step.

www.ingramcontent.com/pod-product-compliance
Lightning Source LLC
Chambersburg PA
CBHW070152230526
45471CB00002B/632